Dr J Simpson

The Ministry of Jesus Christ

A Handbook for Successful Christian Service

Trevor Newport

Life Changing Ministries

Life Changing Ministries

Bemersley House
Gitana Street
Hanley
Stoke on Trent
ST1 1DY
UK

ISBN: 1 874367 50 7

Typeset by CRB Associates, Lenwade, Norwich.
Printed in England by Clays Ltd, St Ives plc.

Contents

Chapter 1

A Ministry of Compassion, Not Sympathy

The ministry of Jesus Christ as seen in the gospels demonstrates the active love that God has for people. One of the words that we see regularly in the gospels is compassion. In fact, compassion is mentioned 42 times in the Bible in total. However, sympathy is **never** mentioned! We never read of Jesus meeting a sick person and showing sympathy by saying something like this: 'I am really sorry for the condition that you have but there is nothing that I can do.' Jesus always operates in compassion and has an answer for **everybody** who is in need and who comes in faith.

It is about time the Church of Jesus Christ stopped operating in sympathy and learned to walk in Holy Spirit anointed compassion. Matthew 14:14 says:

> *'And Jesus went forth, and saw a great multitude, and was moved with **compassion** toward them, and He **healed** their sick.'*

The power of God to heal is the same today as it has

always been and the healing virtue that flows through Jesus Christ is still available today. So many Christians today are hurting because of disease, sickness and aches and pains which Satan has placed upon them. The Church of Jesus Christ should be a place where sick people get healed. Satan is the one who gives sickness. Jesus is the healer. The Word of God declares that *'by His stripes ye were healed'* (1 Peter 2:24). Jesus Christ has already paid the price for all sickness and disease, and all aches and pains. All we have to do is believe in simple faith and be healed.

The Word of God also says that those who believe *'shall lay their hands on the sick and, **they shall recover'*** (Mk 16:18). That is a positive statement. Every time I pray for a sick person I expect them to recover, simply because this Scripture says it.

When I first began praying for the sick about 16 years ago I knew very little. I did not see everybody healed straightaway. However, this does not change God's Word. Over the years I have learnt much about healing and I go on learning every time I pray for people. The Holy Spirit leads you as you step out in faith and expect results.

In Matthew 15:32–38 we have the famous story of how Jesus fed the multitude with seven loaves and a few fish. Notice in verse 32 it says:

> *'I have **compassion** on the multitude because they continue with me now three days, and have nothing to eat: and I will not send them away fasting, lest they faint in the way.'*

We see here how Jesus ministered to peoples' physical needs; i.e. food. God is interested in every area of life and His Word says *'I am the Lord that healeth thee'* (Ex 15:26), and it also says *'But my God shall supply all* *your needs according to **His riches in glory** by Christ Jesus'* (Phil 4:19).

We are also commanded by the Lord to show the same kind of compassion to those in need. 1 John 3:17 says:

> *'But whoso hath this world's good and seeth his brother have need, and shutteth up his bowels of compassion from him, how dwelleth the love of God in him?'*

We have a responsibility to give and to show compassion. There are two ways that this must happen in the Body of Christ; by natural revelation and supernatural revelation. Natural revelation means that if we find out that someone has need of something then we are required scripturally to meet that need if we are able to. Secondly, supernatural revelation happens when God lays upon your heart to give someone something: money, food, clothing, cars etc., and you do it and trust God. I have always found that God has blessed us so much by obeying that 'still small voice' in giving. I remember going to a minister's meeting once and I only had two five pound notes in my wallet. We had no food at home and no more money; we were trusting God. While I was at the meeting the Lord spoke to me and said 'Give five pounds to John.' I had learnt to obey His voice by now and reached into my wallet and gave him £5. Apparently, he had no money at all for his family and so we both went away rejoicing. One hour later when I arrived home there was a cheque in the post for £100. Twenty times what I had given. Hallelujah! God multiplies the seeds that we sow in faith. Because I had shown compassion, the Lord rewarded me for being faithful.

I really believe that it is our duty as serious believers in Christ to seek God with all our might to find the keys to help hurting people. The Word of God says:

'We then that are strong ought to bear the infirmities of the weak, and not to please ourselves.' (Rom 15:1)

Anyone who has sought a healing ministry quickly realises that there is an awesome cost involved. This means regularly fasting (Is 58:3–12; Lk 4:1–14; Mk 9:29), much time spent studying and meditating God's Word (2 Tim 3:14–17; Ps 119:105), and applying God's Word to your own life first. I have been amazed at how many times people have been able to pray the prayer of faith for someone else but have been unable to receive healing for themselves! This surely needs to be addressed first. If we cannot apply the Word of God to our own life then we should not be ministering to others. The main reason why people find difficulty receiving for themselves in the area of healing, is unbelief. A way to deal with this is to get all the scriptures on healing and speak them out aloud over yourselves until faith rises in your heart for yourself. Repentance from unbelief is often necessary as well. (See Mt 13:58; 17:20; Mk 6:6; 9:24; 16:14; Heb 3:12, 19; 4:6, 11.) If a person has a major problem with unbelief then deliverance from a spirit of unbelief is often needed. The way to keep unbelief out of our lives is to keep God's Word before our eyes regularly and to maintain joy in our hearts at all times. Constant praise to God is a vital ingredient to maintaining a victorious life in Christ Jesus (Ps 34:1; Phil 4:4; Heb 13:15). If you are not used to constant praise here on earth then you will be in for a shock when you get to heaven!

*'And the four beasts had each of them six wings about him; and they were full of eyes within: and they **rest not day and night**, saying **holy, holy, holy,** Lord God Almighty, which was, and is, and is to come.'*

(Rev 4:8)

Paul the apostle knew how important it was for him to maintain an attitude of gratitude in his ministry. He wrote:

> *'As unknown, and yet well known; as dying, and behold, we live; as chastened, and not killed; As sorrowful, **yet always rejoicing**; as poor, yet making many rich; as having nothing, and yet possessing all things.'* (2 Cor 6:9–10)

Paul was always being confronted by strong opposition from Satan in some form or another, and yet he spoke more about joy, praise and rejoicing than even King David, and he had definitely discovered this key to victory in God's army.

In the ministry of Jesus Christ we also see that He has compassion and not sympathy towards people who are bound by evil spirits. Look at what Jesus says to Legion after he was delivered, *'... Go home to thy friends, and tell them how great things the Lord hath done for thee, and hath had **compassion** on thee'* (Mk 5:19). One thing that is very clear about Jesus' ministry is that He cast out demons wherever He went and He did not need to look for them. They recognised His authority everywhere He went. I have been involved in casting out devils for about 15 years now and have never gone looking for them. In fact, people who are bound by evil spirits come looking for me! The Word of God says about Jesus' earthly ministry:

> *'And Jesus, when He came out, saw much people, and was moved with **compassion** toward them, because they were as sheep not having a shepherd; and he **began to teach** them many things.'* (Mk 6:34)

Jesus spent much of His ministry teaching people the 'How to's' of living and gave people simple instructions on how to lead a victorious life in the power of the Spirit.

Unless people are taught what the Word of God says they will lead defeated lives and be thwarted by Satan and his cohorts. This is why an essential part of the Body of Christ's ministry today should be to equip the saints to lead victorious lives by faith in God's Word. Sadly, this is not the case in many churches since there seems to be a dearth of Bible teachers with the divine ability to teach revelation knowledge of God's Word to produce overcomers in this life, instead of the overcome. Paul the apostle says in Rom 5:17:

> *'For if by one man's offence death reigned by one: much more they which receive abundance of grace and of the gift of righteousness shall **reign in life** by one, **Jesus Christ**.'*

The Greek says, 'reign as kings in life by one Jesus Christ.' We should overcome every onslaught of the evil one without backing off. No soldier should turn his back on his enemy, or he is likely to be shot in the back! We are called to go from victory to victory; not from one defeat to the next. We need to pray that God will raise up many teachers today who can teach the simple truths of God's Word for the whole man thus producing in the Spirit, a strong and militant body of believers.

Another area of compassion that Jesus taught is found in the famous story of the Good Samaritan (see Lk 10:30–37). In this story Jesus reveals the hardness of people's hearts and the hypocrisy and selfishness towards a man who was in obvious need as he lay in the road. Verse 33 says:

*'But a certain Samaritan, as he journeyed, came where he was: and when he saw him he had **compassion** on him.'*

Doubtless this Samaritan was just as busy as the others with just as many pressing engagements as the priest and the Levite. However, he went out of his way to make sure that this man was well cared for. To emphasise His teaching, Jesus then makes this strong statement in verse 37: *'Go, and do thou likewise.'* The difference between compassion and sympathy is clearly defined here as the Samaritan **did something** to help the man.

If we desire earnestly to live our Christian lives here on earth with maximum results then we need to show compassion towards people.

1.   Those who are sick should be healed.
2.   Those who are in need should be provided for.
3.   Those who are defeated need to be taught.
4.   Those who are bound should be delivered.
5.   Those who are hurting need to be cared for.

God help us all to fulfil our God-given duty to assist mankind to the full.

Chapter 2

A Ministry to People

As we examine the life and ministry of Jesus Christ in His earthly walk we can see that His prime concern is towards **people**. He loves people and is always seen helping them where they are hurting. One of the amazing things that really thrills my heart about the ministry of Jesus Christ is that He **always has time for individuals**. Even when the crowds are thronging Him or awaiting Him at the next venue, He will still come aside and spend time with individual people who are sick, blind or bound by evil spirits.

However, He never seems as if He is in a hurry! He has only three and a half years to fulfil His calling on earth and still He never complains about lack of time. Striving is certainly not a characteristic of the ministry of Jesus.

Let us now pick out some instances in Luke's gospel (chapter 4), and see just how much Jesus maintains His person-to-person link with humanity. Jesus spends 40 days in fasting and prayer in preparation for His ministry and then goes to Nazareth, where He was brought up.

From the outset Satan tries to abort His ministry, because the people; '... *thrust Him out of the city, and led Him unto the brow of the hill whereon their city was built,*

that they might cast Him down headlong.' What a wonderful reception for the Son of God! He announces Himself
and tells them of His mission (verses 18 and 19) and they
try to kill Him. Verse 30 goes on to say:

> *'But He passing through the midst of them went His
> way.'*

This is probably one of the most incredible stories of
divine protection ever written. It seems that there was an
invisible force-field surrounding Jesus so that the mob
could not even touch Him. No doubt He was enclosed
by many strong angels to protect Him. I am glad that we
too have such angelic protection (Heb 1:14; Ps 34:7).

Jesus demonstrates here that even though He has a
tremendous love and compassion for people, He isn't
about to be trampled underfoot by them! You will also
notice a total absence of fear of people. The Word does
say:

> *'The fear of man brings a snare, but whoso putteth his
> trust in the Lord shall be safe* (or shall be set on
> high).'   (Prov 29:25)

Jesus gives these people at Nazareth an opportunity to
experience the love and power of God for themselves,
but by rejecting Jesus they refuse something that would
have blessed them not only in this life but for all eternity.
If only they had realised what they were doing.

In Luke 4:31–37 we see Jesus entering the Synagogue
at Capernaum. He taught the people with an authority
which causes great astonishment. In this same meeting a
man begins to shout with a loud voice. I am quite sure
that everyone's head begins to turn and look at this dis-
turbance since it wasn't the norm in the Synagogue! The
very presence of Jesus causes an unclean spirit within the

man to scream and shout, and we see throughout the gospels that this is quite a common occurrence when Jesus begins ministering. Demons recognise authority! Obviously this man is in need of deliverance from the unclean spirit and we see the compassion of Jesus as He commands the spirit to be quiet and to come out of the man. This phenomenon still happens in churches today where people who are bound by evil spirits begin to cry out for deliverance. In many cases, they are told to stop getting excited and to calm down. This is very sad. I was pastoring a church once and the deacons came up to me after a service and told me that for the previous 20 years or so they had experienced a problem in their meetings. Every time the Holy Spirit began to move in worship, certain people would begin shouting and crying out with loud voices, just like the man in this story. I told them that it would be dealt with in six months. Praise God that in five months all the screams had gone. Jesus might have ignored this problem and told the man to settle down and stop disturbing the meeting, but we never see Jesus treat anybody in this way. He cares for people whatever the problem. It is the duty of the Church to care for any individual who is broken, wounded and hurting. I am glad that the gospel of Jesus Christ includes all that we need to make people whole in body, soul and spirit, through teaching the Word, worship and the nine-fold gifts of the Holy Spirit. Instead of this man going back to his home in further torment he was free to lead a normal life.

Wherever Jesus was there was always work to do. In verse 38 of Luke 4 Jesus apparently goes for a meal with Simon. His mother-in-law has been taken ill with a great fever. Jesus was probably advised not to eat there in case He caught the same affliction, but there was obviously faith in the house because they asked Him to help her (verse 38). We can see the absolute simplicity of Jesus because He rebuked the fever and it left her. Hallelujah! The healing was so complete that she was well enough to minister to them (probably by serving a hearty meal).

This story shows how close Jesus comes to people. So close that they can touch Him. He does not act high and mighty and stand aloof from people like the Scribes and Pharisees, but rather He mixes with people, and communes with them, and shows them He cares.

In Luke 5:4-11 we see an interesting situation in Jesus' dealings with Simon (Jesus had a lot of dealings with him). Simon had been striving all night to catch fish and had caught nothing. I am sure that at this point he must have felt tired and discouraged and was probably feeling sorry for himself. Jesus demonstrates how much He cares for every part of our lives, when He performed a tremendous miracle for Simon. This has an incredible effect on all of them present. Simon demonstrates sound faith in Jesus by saying:

> *'Master, we have toiled all the night, and have taken nothing: nevertheless at thy word I will let down the net.'*

We don't see him moan or complain! He seemingly just does what Jesus tells him to do. It is often when we have tried and exhausted all earthly methods, that we are then in a place to respond to divine instructions. We would all be much better off if we spent the time seeking God first to find out what it is He wants us to do. We would grow far faster towards the high calling of God for our lives and be far less hassled on our journey. One instruction from Jesus produced a multitude of fishes! So much so that their nets started to break. I am sure that Simon never forgot this incident.

There are so many spiritual truths in this episode. Not only do their nets break but they fill both ships which begin to sink! The biggest catch in history! We should always obey the instructions of Jesus straight-away. It pays to **obey**. This incident has a dramatic effect on Simon Peter. He falls at Jesus' knees and says to Him, *'Depart from me: for I am a sinful man, O Lord'* (verse 8). The Holy presence of God comes through this miracle and shows Peter up for what he is: full of sin and fear.

Jesus ministers individually to Simon once again and encourages him by saying:

> *'Fear not; from henceforth thou shalt catch men.'*
> (verse 10)

Jesus is beginning to build His team of disciples and would-be apostles and He never gives up on Peter. Jesus knows that Peter, like us, can change and become useful in the Kingdom. I am glad that Jesus is patient and **long-suffering** to us. He does not choose Peter for what he is but for **what he could become**! We are never chosen because of our abilities, strengths or gifts, we are usually chosen because we have simply made ourselves available. It may take a long time before you are ready to be used in God's service but let me encourage you by saying that **God is more patient than we are**! Most people would have given up on Peter five times over and said that he would never come to much. Jesus believes that Peter will change and he does! Jesus tells Peter on one occasion:

> *'Thou art Simon the son of Jona; thou shalt be called Cephas...'* (Jn 1:42)

The word Simon actually means 'a shaky reed'. In other words, even the simplest of winds could blow him over. However, Cephas means Peter, or a stone. A stone is solid, firm and dependable. Jesus knows that Simon is no good for divine service in his present state but, here is the good news! Simon, you will be **'a stone'**. Unlike the religious Pharisees, Simon does change and becomes a powerful man of God. However shaky you may be now, God can change you and shape you into the person that Jesus wants you to be to serve Him in the Body of Christ and bring glory to Him. Often we see Jesus having personal confrontations with His immediate staff and picking them up when they are down or correcting their wrong ideas. This particular incident with Peter, James and John, results in all three of them at the same time being called by Jesus to be catchers of men instead of fish! Verse 11 says:

> *'. . . they forsook all, and followed Him.'*

One minute Peter is on his knees trembling in fear and begging Jesus to depart from him, the next he is in full-time service for the Lord, even giving up his now lucrative job as a fisherman! I wonder if the temptation was there for him to stay as a fisherman now that his business had turned around overnight. We don't actually see any hesitancy in Peter. It seems that he followed Jesus immediately.

In Luke 5:12–14 we see Jesus entering a city where He meets a man who is full of leprosy. (See Leviticus 13 for a complete study regarding leprosy.) Notice it says *'full of leprosy'* which means that he would have dwelt outside the camp, and would have been forbidden contact with other people in case the leprosy spread. Jesus knew all of this and yet it does not concern Him. Verse 13 says:

> *'And He put forth His hand and **touched him**, saying, "I will: be thou clean." And immediately the leprosy departed from him.'*

Jesus touches him! Isn't He afraid of catching this dreaded skin disease Himself? Of course not. Jesus Christ is the great **I AM** of the Bible! In Exodus 15:26 God says: *'I AM the LORD that healeth thee.'*

Jesus Christ is God Almighty in the flesh who comes to bring divine healing and health to His people. Whenever Jesus comes near sickness and disease it disappears rather quickly. Once we become established in the Word of God for ourselves regarding divine healing, we can be just as confident as Jesus was towards sick people. Jesus says:

> *'He that believeth on me the works that I do shall he do also: and greater works than these shall he do: because I go unto my Father.'* (Jn 14:12)

What an amazing statement. The first time I read that Scripture I did not believe it at all. Over the months, however, as I absorbed God's powerful Word into my spirit all my unbelief began to be replaced by **faith**. I came to the point in my life where I believed that I could do the same miracles as Jesus in **His** name alone, and once I believed I began to see small healings to begin with. Over the years God has moved me on one step at a time. He is constantly teaching me as I step out in faith and believe that He can use me (Mk 16:15–20). This precious man who was full of leprosy, an outcast from society, finds himself totally healed in a moment of time! Just imagine what this did to his entire life. He could mix with people again, hold down a job, visit relatives, go to the market. This man's meeting with Jesus is one he will never forget! Jesus knows the power of personal ministry on an individual basis. Even though Jesus was rapidly becoming a well-known evangelist He always had time for the individual! Those of use who are called to preach must always keep this particular example of Jesus before us or else we will lose the ability to relate to people.

The next story in Luke 5:18–26 really drives home the fact that Jesus doesn't want to leave anybody out! Here we have a group of men who care very much for their friend and obviously have the faith to believe that Jesus can heal him. However, they have one big problem. The house where the meeting is being held is full. Some people at this point would have said: 'It must not be God's will to heal you. Let's go home!'

Some people have done that and stayed sick. What would you have done? Real faith stops at nothing and never gives up even if the door seems to be tightly shut. These men are so determined that they actually climb up onto the roof and make a large hole in the roof; large enough to lower the man and his couch down into the room (verse 19). One can imagine the crowd inside the house gazing upwards at this astonishing sight. The determination of his friends pays off because Jesus apparently sees him immediately and says: *'Man thy sins are forgiven thee'* (verse 20).

Notice Jesus sees *'**their** faith'* (verse 20). Their faith is demonstrated by their actions! No wonder James says: *'faith without works is dead'* (James 2:20, 26).

Jesus forgives the man his sins and heals him. It is highly probable that forgiveness and the healing is linked as sin often hinders people from being healed. We see a very important lesson here. Everybody else sees only the man's palsy but Jesus sees his sin! Jesus came primarily to cleanse us from sin which is obviously far more important than a healthy body. You can go to heaven with a sick body, but not with a sick soul. Sin needs to be cleansed. Thank God that:

> *'the blood of Jesus Christ His Son cleanseth us from all sin.'* (1 Jn 1:7)

I am glad that we do not have to choose between one or the other, as God's Word clearly states in Psalm 103:2–3:

> *'Bless the Lord, O my soul, and forget not all his benefits: who forgiveth **all thine iniquities**; who **healeth all thy diseases.**'*

In this particular story Jesus both forgives the man's sins, and heals him of the palsy. (Palsy means to be paralysed or to lose use of part of the body.)

In the next story in Luke 5:27–32 Jesus calls Levi into His service when He says *'Follow me'* (verse 27). Levi then holds a great feast in his own house and invites his fellow publicans. Jesus sits down and eats with them. We see Him continuing His practice of getting down to where the people are. Jesus immediately comes under criticism from the self-righteous Pharisees who say to Him:

> *'Why do ye eat and drink with publicans and sinners?'*
> (verse 30)

Jesus once again exposes their hypocrisy by saying:

> *'They that are whole need not a physician; but they that are sick. I came not to call the righteous, but sinners to repentance.'*   (verses 31, 32)

Jesus says this because He knows that only those who recognise their sinful condition can get saved whereas those who think that they are alright do not recognise their need of a saviour. As Christians we need to pray for unsaved people to have a revelation of their sin and so realise their need to be cleansed of it. That is why prayer, intercession and spiritual warfare against the powers of darkness are so important, because 2 Cor 4:4 says:

> *'In whom the god of this world* (Satan) *hath blinded the minds of them which believe not, lest the **light of the glorious gospel of Christ**, who is the image of God, **should shine unto them**.'*

In the following encounter, found in Luke 6:1–5, Jesus demonstrates His infinite patience even with the Pharisees. As usual, they are picking fault and criticising the disciples of Jesus concerning their petty rules and regulations. The disciples of Jesus are walking through a corn field and simply plucking the corn, rubbing it in their hands and eating it. Patiently and gently (on this occasion), Jesus teaches them not to be legalistic on the Sabbath day by saying *'that the Son of man is Lord also of the Sabbath'* (verse 5). Jesus knows that even some of the Pharisees will be converted and serve Him faithfully one day. Nicodemus who is a ruler of the Jews, comes to Jesus (Jn 3:1–13; see also Jn 7:50 and Jn 19:39), which strongly suggests a keen interest and possible conversion to Christ. Read through these Scriptures in John's Gospel and see how sincere Nicodemus is with his enquiries and comments about Jesus. Also in Acts 6:7 we read:

> *'And the word of God increased; and the number of the disciples multiplied in Jerusalem greatly; and a **great company of the priests were obedient to the faith**.'*

Maybe Nicodemus was among them. Jesus even cares about Pharisees knowing that even they can change from their stubborn, religious, hypocritical ways. Thank God that He is a God of mercy!

The next story of the man with the withered hand, is well-known (Lk 6:6–11). Here we see Jesus caring more for the precious man than He does for His own reputation! No doubt this man could not work in proper employment and probably had difficulty in washing, dressing, eating and caring for himself. Every part of this man's life must have been affected by this withered hand. How much we take our hands for granted.

Jesus knows what will happen when He heals the man. Sometimes we compromise because we fear what other people will think of us. This is sin! The Bible says:

> *'The **fear of man** bringeth a snare: but whoso putteth his trust in the LORD shall be safe.'* (Prov 29:25)

Jesus addresses the religious crowd and says:

> *'... I will ask you one thing; Is it lawful on the sabbath days to do good, or to do evil? to save life, or to destroy it?'* (Lk 6:9)

The reaction is instantaneous! As soon as Jesus issues the command, *'stretch forth thy hand'* (verse 19) and his hand is restored perfectly like the other one, the crowd goes wild. Verse 11 says:

> *'And they were filled with madness; and communed one with another what they might do to Jesus.'*

This story should really straighten us out when it comes to obeying God. Whatever criticism we invoke; whatever anybody says about us; and however much we suffer for serving the Lord we must **obey at all cost** and **never compromise, water down** or **back off** from **doing the will of God with all of our hearts. It pays to obey!**

Remember Saul in the Old Testament? (1 Sam 15).

God gives Saul one last chance to prove himself before removing him from being king. Samuel comes to Saul and says:

> *'Now go and smite Amalek and utterly destroy all that they have, and spare them not...'* (verse 3)

Verse 9 goes on to say:

> *'But Saul and the people spared Agag, and the best of the sheep, and of the oxen, and of the fatlings, and the lambs, and all that was good, and would not utterly destroy them...'*

Saul completely loses his last chance through disobedience. God sends Samuel to Saul and rebukes him with these now famous and awesome words:

> *'Hath the Lord as great delight in burnt offerings and sacrifices as in obeying the voice of the Lord? Behold, to **obey** is better than sacrifice, and to hearken than the fat of rams. For **rebellion is as the sin of witchcraft**, and **stubborness** is as iniquity and idolatry, because thou hast rejected the word of the Lord, he hath also rejected thee from being king.'*
>
> (verses 22–23)

Jesus never falters or wavers in His obedience to the Father's will. The only time that we see the humanity of Jesus Christ is in the garden when He finally declares:

> *'...not my will but Thine be done.'* (Lk 22:42)

In the ministry of Jesus Christ towards people we see that He never considers His own life, or reputation as meaning anything to Him. People are His number one priority. Even as His ministry grows and becomes widespread Jesus is just as caring, thoughtful and compassionate towards the needs of people. What an example to follow! People are the most important commodity. Jesus has left us the finest example of self-sacrifice, care, love and obedience. The Word says in 1 Jn 2:6:

> *'He that saith he abideth in Him* (Christ) *ought himself also so to walk, **even as He walked**.'*

Let us follow His example and love people as Jesus did, by laying down our lives also.

Chapter 3

A Ministry of Physical Healing

Introduction

The subject of Divine Healing is often confused with many present-day counterfeits. The satanic view held by Christian Scientists, for example, is that there is no sin or sickness. It is all in the mind. However, the Bible makes it clear that there is sickness and disease as a result of original sin. As we accept the whole truth of the Bible, it will become abundantly clear that the church and the world need Divine Healing. Probably the reason why Christian Scientists have gone so far astray is because they only accept fifty percent of the Bible. G.C. Bevington remarks on the subject:

> 'Divine Healing is not imaginary. It is not simply the exercise of will power. It is not mind cure. It is not spiritualism. It is not immunity from death or from sickness, as those who believe in Divine Healing get sick; and when their work is done they die. It is not mere presumption nor a disregard of God's will. It is the direct power of God upon the body.'

Divine Healing is just as much for today as it was in the days of Jesus. The time when miracles, healing and the gifts of the Spirit in general will cease is when we no longer need them when, of course, we are made perfect (1 Cor 13:8–12; 1 Jn 3:2).

It will be proved indisputably from God's Word that Divine Healing is for everybody. However, there are several reasons why some people do not get healed and this will be looked at from a scriptural standpoint.

It must be made very clear right from the beginning exactly what constitutes Divine Healing. The biblical definition, as we shall prove, can be summarised as:

> The direct power of God by the Holy Spirit upon a person to heal completely without any medical aid, potions or operations.

Jesus is the Healer

In Matthew's Gospel we have the following record:

> *'And **Jesus** went about all Galilee, teaching in their synagogues, and preaching the gospel of the Kingdom, and **healing all manner of sickness and all manner of disease** among the people.'*
> (Mt 4:23; 8–3, 16; 9:35; 12:13, 22; 14:36; 15:30; Mk 10:52; Lk 7:21; 17:14; Jn 4:50; 9:6)

And Luke records:

> *'How God anointed **Jesus** of Nazareth with the Holy Ghost and with power; who went about doing good, and **healing all that were oppressed of the devil**; for God was with Him.'*   (Acts 10:38)

As the gospels are read at the beginning of the New Testament there are frequent occasions when Jesus

26

demonstrates the power of God to heal the sick and to deliver from demon power. In fact, someone once quoted that two-thirds of the ministry of Jesus was spent in healing and delivering. The question may be asked 'Was this power to heal the sick only intended while Jesus was on the earth to set up His Kingdom?' This is certainly a reasonable question, but the Bible has the very definite answer of no! The book of Hebrews states:

> *'Jesus Christ the same yesterday, and today, and for ever.'* (Heb 13:8)

This is a most interesting statement and if we look closely enough at the Old Testament we can see that Jesus is mentioned throughout as the Healer. Firstly, Jesus declares Himself as the great I AM:

> *'Jesus said unto them, Verily, verily, I say unto you, Before Abraham was, I am.'* (Jn 8:58)

If we turn to the book of Exodus we can now see Jesus clearly:

> *'And God said unto Moses, I AM THAT I AM: and He said, Thus shalt thou say unto the children of Israel, I AM hath sent me unto you.'* (Ex 3:14)

Jesus is consequently the great I AM of the entire Bible (Jn 6:35, 41, 48, 51; 8:12, 23, 24, 28; 9:5; 10:7, 9, 11, 14; 11:25; 13:13, 19; 14:6; 15:1; 18:5, 8; Rev 1:8, 18).

With regard to Divine Healing in the Old Testament we can see Jesus revealed clearly in the book of Exodus:

> *'... If thou wilt diligently hearken to the voice of the LORD thy God, and wilt do that which is right in His sight, and wilt give ear to His commandments, and*

*keep all His statutes, I will put none of these diseases upon thee, which I have brought upon the Egyptians: for **I AM the LORD that healeth thee**.'*

(Ex 15:26; Deut 7:15; Mal 4:2)

In this verse we see two of the persons of the triune Godhead. Firstly, God the Father is talked about by the speaker and then the speaker is also revealed as 'The Lord' who is obviously Jesus because of the phrase 'I AM'. So we can see that all healings that took place in the Old Testament were performed by Jesus; e.g. Hezekiah (2 Kings 20:1–11) and Naaman by Elisha (2 Kings 5).

We have thus proved that Divine Healing by the Lord Jesus was for 'yesterday' under the Old Testament. It was also 'today' during Christ's ministry. We shall now prove that when Jesus went back to heaven His healing power was still on the earth.

Jesus says just before He leaves earth:

*'And these signs shall follow them that believe; **in my name shall they cast out devils ... they shall lay hands on the sick, and they shall recover**.'*　　(Mk 16:17, 18)

Jesus also says:

'Verily, verily, I say unto you, He that believeth on me, the works that I do shall he do also; and greater works than these shall he do; because I go unto my Father.'　　(Jn 14:12)

From these two statements alone we see that Divine Healing and other miracles are to be continued. Jesus says, *'In my name'* shall healings take place. The fact is that the Name of Jesus is just as powerful now as if Jesus were actually on the earth today. The mention of God's

name was special in the Old Testament (Job 1:21; Ps
5:11; 7:17; 8:1,9; 20:1,5; 33:21; 52:9; 54:1; 74:7; 86:9
etc.). We have such phrases as *'blessed be the name of the
Lord'* and *'how excellent is thy name in all the earth'*. The
emphasis is upon His name. The same principle applies
in the New Covenant. The Children of God are saved,
healed and made completely whole *'in the Name of
Jesus'*. As the book of Acts is read it is clear that the
identical healings and miracles that Jesus performs are
evidenced in exactly the same way apart from the fact
that the apostles use the Name of Jesus. Shortly after
Pentecost (Acts 2) we have a wonderful example of Jesus
healing *'a certain man lame from his mother's womb'*
(Acts 3:2) through Peter the apostle. Peter uses the
words:

> *'In the **name of Jesus Christ of Nazareth** rise up and
> walk.'*   (Acts 3:6)

Needless to say the man is completely healed and is so
excited he is seen *'walking, and leaping and praising God'*.
Notice that he gives God the glory because it is God
(Jesus) who performs the miracle. Paul the apostle
acknowledges who it is that does the working and who
deserves the glory:

> *'... which is Christ in you, the hope of glory ...
> whereunto I also labour, striving according to his
> working, which worketh in me mightily.'*
> (Col 1:27, 29)

All the way through the Acts of the Apostles there are
miraculous instances of healings and deliverances all
executed *'in the name of Jesus'* (5:16; 14:10; 16:18; 19:12;
28:8). The best example to prove that the Lord Jesus
Christ performs the healings is the instance when Peter

goes to Lydda and meets a man called Aeneas and says to him:

> *'**Jesus Christ** maketh thee whole.'* (Acts 9:34)

Also countless millions of people throughout the last two thousand years, particularly this century, have been miraculously healed by the use of the Name of Jesus. In crusades people are prayed for by the laying on of hands, and also Christians who are sick claim Divine Healing in the Name of Jesus on their own and they are healed. This proves the words of Jesus:

> *'And whatsoever ye shall ask **in my name**, that will I do, that the Father may be glorified in the son. If ye shall ask **anything in my name**, I will do it.'*
>
> (Jn 14:13, 14)

Consequently, we have proved that Jesus Christ was the Healer under the Old Covenant; Jesus was the Healer on the earth; and Jesus is the Healer today for all who are obedient to God.

Divine Healing is Part of Salvation

In the Old Testament there are basically four Hebrew words used for salvation. All of them either state or strongly imply healing. For instance *'yeshuwah'* can be translated deliverance, health, salvation, saving (health) and welfare; also *'yeshuwah'* can be translated rescue (naturally or spiritually), deliverance, help and safety. So there is plenty of evidence to suggest that salvation is not just deliverance from sin but sickness also. In the New Testament it is almost exactly the same with the Greek word *'soteria'* which can be translated deliver, health, salvation and save.

When the Lord Jesus Christ died on the cross He was made sin for us (Is 53:6; Rom 8:3; 2 Cor 5:21) by carrying all our sins, iniquities and transgressions. This is a very well-known fact that nobody would ever dispute. Neither would anybody dispute that all our sins can be forgiven through true repentance (1 Jn 1:7, 9). However, the teaching that is sadly neglected about Calvary, is that Jesus bore all our sicknesses, pains, diseases and mental problems as well (Is 53:4 with Mt 8:17; Is 53:5 and 1 Pet 2:24).

The Hebrew word for 'griefs' in Isaiah 53:4 is *'cholly'* which can equally be translated disease or sicknesses. Consequently, the believer has just as much right to claim Divine Healing as he does forgiveness for his sins. An interesting observation throughout the Bible is that sin and sickness appear together regularly. For instance in Psalm 103:3:

> *'Who forgiveth all thine iniquities; who healeth all thy diseases.'*
>   (see also Is 33:24; 53:4–6; Lk 5:20–24; Jas 5:15)

In the third epistle of John also we have the revealing statement absolutely justifying not only Divine Healing but moreover Divine Health:

> *'Beloved, I wish above all things that thou mayest prosper, and be in health, even as thy soul prospereth.'*
>   (3 Jn 2)

It is therefore clear that God means every child of God to be an overcomer in every realm; a victor over the devil. The full message of the gospel includes Divine Healing just as much as freedom from the dominion of sin. A statement in the book of Hebrews sums up this fact:

> *'Wherefore He is able also to save* (heal, preserve, make whole) *them to the uttermost that come unto God by Him, seeing He ever liveth to make intercession for them.'*
> (Heb 7:25)

Every Christian has the capacity to be made *'every whit whole'* (Jn 7:23). It is part of redemption, it is part of the finished work of the cross. Consequently there is never any need to pray to ask God if it is His will to heal. **It is always God's will to heal.** Even if death itself happens we should believe God to raise the dead. God has given us power over death itself in the Name of Jesus.

The Bible gives us an example to illustrate this point. Hezekiah is *'sick unto death'* (2 Kings 20:1) and Isaiah actually prophesies the death of Hezekiah. He says:

> *'Thus saith the Lord, set thine house in order; for thou shalt die, and not live.'*

Hezekiah then pleads with the Lord and the most remarkable thing happens. The Lord actually heals Hezekiah and adds fifteen years on to his life (verses 5, 6). Another example is when The Lord passes judgement upon the child of Bathsheba. David fasts and intercedes for the child (2 Sam 12:13–21). In verse 22 we have the declaration by David:

> *'... who can tell whether God will be gracious to me, that the child may live?'*

Consequently, we cannot know if God will be gracious. Therefore, we are always to believe for total healing.

Also, another aspect of the salvation found in Christ is to redeem us from the curse of the law (Gal 3:13). Jesus was actually cursed for mankind which included the momentary rejection by His Father (Mt 27:46). This was because Jesus was carrying the sin, sickness, problems, burdens and anxieties of the whole world. He did this to make men and women *'new creations'* (2 Cor 5:17) and to become *'partakers of the Divine Nature'* (2 Pet 1:4). The old nature is full of sin, disease and weakness. The new creation in Christ is full of freedom, liberty, health and good fruits (compare Gal 5:19–21 with Gal 5:22–23). Consequently, it cannot be emphasised enough that God means all His children to be well. The following verses in John's first epistle are most applicable here:

> *'And this is the confidence that we have in Him, that, if we ask any thing according to His will, He heareth us: And if we know that He hear us, whatsoever we ask, we know that we have the petitions that we desired of Him.'*   (1 Jn 5:14–15)

Therefore, since we know for sure that it is God's will to heal us we are always confident concerning the physical manifestation of healing.

Divine Healing by Faith

The Bible says:

> *'But without faith it is impossible to please Him; for he that cometh to God must believe that He is, and that He is a rewarder of them that diligently seek Him.'*   (Heb 11:6)

The Bible also says:

> *'. . . for whatsoever is not of faith is sin.'*
>   (Rom 14:23)

33

As we study God's Word it is very clear that God has predestined one means by which men and women receive from God. That way is **faith**. Faith is the only channel that will move God to do anything. A person becomes a Christian by faith (Rom 4:16; Eph 2:8). When a person is baptised in the Holy Spirit it will only happen by faith (Gal 3:2, 5, 14). It is just the same with Divine Healing. God cannot heal where faith is not operating as Mark records:

> *'He* (Jesus) *could there do no mighty works, save that He laid His hands upon a few sick folk, and healed them.'* (Mk 6:5)

Wherever Jesus went He always had the power to heal. It merely depended upon whether or not the people decided to use their faith. Throughout the gospels we read phrases like *'thy faith hath made thee whole'* (Mt 9:22); *'According to your faith be it unto you'* (Mt 9:29); *'thy faith hath saved thee'* (Lk 18:42) all of which were physical healings. Also after Jesus' death, resurrection and ascension we have the same rule applying in the Acts of the Apostles. Paul met a man who was a cripple from his mother's womb and Luke says:

> *'The same heard Paul speak: who stedfastly beholding him, and perceiving that he had faith to be healed...'* (Acts 14:9)

Thus God's rule still applies today with regard to healing. He *'calleth those things which be not as though they were'* (Rom 4:17). In fact, the main reason why people do not receive their healing is because they do not use faith. This is not always their fault. Sometimes faith has not been taught correctly. Since faith is such an important part of Divine Healing it will be useful to state briefly what faith is. Firstly, faith is not just believing, because *'the devils also believe and tremble'* (Jas 2:19). Faith is defined perfectly in the Bible in Hebrews 11:1:

> *'Now faith is the substance of things hoped for, the evidence of things not seen.'*

To put this into practice we can take heed to Jesus' words:

> *'Have faith in God. For verily I say to you, That whosoever shall say unto this mountain, Be thou removed, and be thou cast into the sea; and shalt not doubt in his heart, but shall believe that those things which he saith shall come to pass; he shall have whatsoever he saith. Therefore, I say unto you, What things soever ye desire, when ye pray, believe that ye receive them, and ye shall have them.'*   (Mk 11:22–24)

These few simple verses tell us all there is to be known about faith. The fact is that faith is simply putting God's Word into action, and trusting Him for the results.

> *'Be ye doers of the word, and not hearers only, deceiving your own selves.'*   (Jas 1:22)

Another way of putting it is claiming God's promise and thanking Him in advance for the answer (Phil 4:6). This is what Paul the apostle means by *'we walk by faith, not by sight'* (2 Cor 5:7). The same principle applies when we repent of a sin in our life. We believe that God forgives us according to His Word and praise Him, even though we may still feel guilty. The way to receive healing is to claim such verses as Ex 15:26; Ps 103:3; Is 53:5 and particularly *'by whose stripes ye **were healed'*** (1 Pet 2:24), and praise God for the healing even though

35

symptoms persist. Personally I can state these facts very boldly because they are my continual experience. God will cause the physical manifestation in His time (Heb 6:12, 15).

Reasons Why Some Fail to Receive Divine Healing

The Bible gives many reasons why God is unable to heal or people are not able to receive their healing. Some people are ignorant concerning God's reliability to fulfil His Word (Jn 8:32, 36). Community unbelief is sometimes a great hindrance (Mt 13:58; Mk 6:5–6). This means that people around may be doubting and talking negatively. This will always create a barrier. That is why it is necessary to teach sound doctrine concerning faith and Divine Healing to remove any doubt. Pride is also a stumbling block to some people. God hates pride (1 Jn 2:15–16) and pride will hinder faith and the Spirit of God from moving (2 Kings 5:12; 2 Chron 32:24–26). It is a fact that *'God resisteth the proud but giveth grace unto the humble'* (Jas 4:6).

We have already mentioned that *'without faith it is impossible to please God'* (Heb 11:6) but this works both ways. It is important that if one person is praying for another person that they both have faith (Mt 9:28; 17:19–20; Jas 5:15–17). If there is unbelief in either party it could result in failure, making it a lot harder to receive healing at some future date. This shows the responsibility upon men with the gifts of healings.

Another reason why Divine Healing is hindered is that sometimes the affliction is the work of a demon (evil spirit) which must be cast out (Mt 9:32–33; 12:22; Mk 9:25–27; Lk 13:11), or because they are continuing in some kind of sin. The Bible is very clear that:

> *'If I regard iniquity in my heart, the Lord will not hear me.'* (Ps 66:18)

This is very true for healing (Num 12:10; 2 Kings 5:27; 2 Chron 26:16–21; Prov 28:13; Mic 6:13; Acts 12:23; 1 Cor 11:27–30; Jas 5:15). Frequently, when the person has repented, the healing is soon manifested. In James 5:8 we are told to:

> *'Draw nigh to God, and He will draw nigh to you.'*

A person seeking Divine Healing may not be healed because of luke-warmness or half-heartedness towards God and His work. This obviously has to be put right (Mt 6:22–24; 8:21; Lk 9:57–62; 16:10–13; Jas 1:6; Rev 3:15–16).

The area of forgiveness is a most important one and sometimes a person may not receive healing simply because they have not forgiven someone (Mt 5:23–24; 18:28–35; Mk 11:25–26; Lk 6:37; 1 Cor 11:30–32).

The Word of God tells us:

> *'If ye forgive not men their trespasses, neither will your Father forgive your trespasses.'* (Mt 6:15)

Another reason why some are not healed is demonstrated in the story of Peter walking on the water. He shows absolute faith when he starts on the water (Mt 14:20–30), but then he looks at the circumstances around him instead of to Jesus who is the *'author and finisher of our faith'* (Heb 12:2). If he had continued as he started, he would have reached Jesus without sinking. People can fail to receive their healing because they waver in their faith and are not consistent (2 Kings 20:2–5; Mt 15:21–28; Lk 5:19–20; Heb 11:6).

Another common reason for doubt is when a person is

not healed immediately. People were healed immediately in Jesus' time (Mt 8:3; 20:34; Mk 1:31, 42; Lk 8:44; Jn 5:9) as many also are today. However, this is not always the case (Mt 8:13; 9:22; 15:28; 17:18; Mk 8:23–25; Jn 4:52; 9:6–7; Heb 6:12–15). Therefore we must never limit God to instant healings only. A similar reason why healings are prevented is when a person seeking healing begins to look out for feelings and symptoms (Rom 4:18–21; 2 Cor 4:18; 5:7; Heb 11:1). This is completely alien to faith and must be guarded against. Some people fail to act in faith upon God's Word and wait for something to take place even though it is there. This is like staying in prison when God has clearly opened the cell doors widely. All we have to do sometimes is walk out of our bondage. This is *'faith with works'* (1 Sam 14:6; Jas 2:14, 17, 18, 20, 22, 26). The fact is that we are to act solely upon the strength of God's Word (1 Sam 17:37; Mt 9:18; 14:36). Others cast away their confidence as soon as testing comes (Heb 1:3; 3:14; 10:35).

One of the reasons why God the Father sent the gift of the Holy Spirit was to impart to the church the full blessings of redemption. Some people fail to recognise this baptism in the Holy Ghost and remain in a weak condition (Rom 8:11; 2 Cor 4:13). Consequently, healing is delayed or never manifested. Simply having an academic head knowledge belief in Divine Healing is also not sufficient to bring about actual miracles of healings (Jas 2:19; 1 Cor 2:4–5; 4:20). We must believe from the heart (Rom 10:9). Many people have all the faith in the world for others to be healed, but when they need healing themselves they find a problem in appropriating the biblical promise of Divine Healing personally (Ex 15:26; 1 Kings 8:56; Ps 103:1–3; Is 53:4–5; Jer 1:12; Mt 8:17; Rom 4:20, 21; 2 Cor 1:20; 5:17; 1 Pet 2:24; 2 Pet 1:4).

Many people have difficulty in believing until they experience and see the physical manifestation (Mk

11:22–24; Jn 20:24–29; 1 Pet 1:8; 1 Jn 5:14–15). The devil is constantly seeking to take people's eyes off faith and the Word of God. We must not be ignorant of the devil's devices (2 Cor 2:11) but rather have on the armour of God (Eph 6:11–18). Also, people tend to base their faith on improvement to their condition rather than in the promise of total healing (Mk 11:22). Our faith and trust are always to be in God and never circumstances or temporal things. Finally, many are thwarted in their quest for healing by listening to unbelieving Christians or traditions of men (Mk 7:13).

The plain fact is that Divine Healing is for every Christian now despite what Satan will say – because Jesus is the same today (Heb 13:8).

Conclusion

We have shown that the Bible clearly states that God wants all His children in health and free from *'the curse of the law'*. We have also shown why some people fail to receive their healing. Too many people base what they believe upon their experience instead of upon the Word of God. If we ever drift away from God's Word in any department of our lives we will find ourselves starved of the blessings that God longs to impart upon His children.

Therefore act upon God's Word and receive your healing today and remember:

>   *'I AM the LORD that healeth thee.'*   (Ex 15:26)

and:

>   *'By His **stripes ye were healed**.'*   (1 Pet 2:24)

Chapter 4

Baptism in the Holy Spirit and Fire

Introduction

When most people give their testimony regarding their salvation it is usual that they have a deep burden and zeal to win others for Christ. God in His infinite wisdom and foreknowledge had predestined before the foundation of the world that the church should be equipped with power to enable it to tell others about the gospel of Jesus Christ without any inferiority, guilt or fear. God knew that conversion itself was not going to give mankind the boldness, authority and complete assurance in preaching the gospel message to the world that it would need in order to make the required impact on people today. Consequently, God prepared a promise to the whole church after conversion to equip it whilst on the earth with fearless power. This power is found in – and only in – the baptism in the Holy Ghost and fire:

> *'Ye shall receive power, after that the Holy Ghost is come upon you.'*   (Acts 1:8)

When dealing with spiritual matters we must always be conscious of not going 'over-board' on certain issues.

Some people have rejected the power of the Holy Spirit and say that it is no longer needed and fill themselves full of the Word of God. On the other hand some people have rejected the Bible and claim that all we need is the Holy Spirit. A careful reading of the Bible makes it abundantly clear that we need to be completely filled with God's Word **and** filled with the Holy Spirit to be able to lead a totally victorious and overcoming life (2 Tim 2:16; 3:16; Heb 4:12; Eph 5:18). As the hymn writer puts it:

'Make me what Thou wouldest have me to be,
Filled with Thy Spirit and filled with Thy Word.'

Jesus spent 30 years on the earth without performing any miracles or mighty works. Then, one day, He tells John the Baptist to baptise Him in water. At the same time Jesus is baptised by the Holy Spirit from heaven. Matthew 3:16 says:

'And Jesus, when He was baptized, went up straightway out of the water: and, lo, the heavens were opened unto Him, and He saw the Spirit of God descending like a dove, and lighting upon Him.'

John the Baptist had just announced the coming of Jesus by saying:

'I indeed baptize you with water unto repentance: but He that cometh after me is mightier than I, whose shoes I am not worthy to bear: He shall baptize you with the Holy Ghost (spirit), *and with fire.'*

(Mt 3:11)

Shortly after this experience, Jesus begins working miracles, signs and wonders.

We shall now make a detailed study of this baptism,

for without it we shall never experience the full ministry of Jesus Christ in our own lives and service for the Lord.

The Baptiser

The Scriptures make it abundantly clear that the Lord Jesus Christ, though in heaven at this present dispensation, is the baptiser with the Holy Ghost and fire. In fact, all four of the gospels tell us plainly that the Lord Jesus Christ is the Holy Spirit baptiser (Mt 3:11; Mk 1:8; Lk 3:16; Jn 1:33). This shows its importance since it is repeated over and over again in Scripture (Gen 41:32). We also see this confirmed yet again by the very lips of Jesus Himself when telling His disciples that the Holy Ghost will be distributed to them when Jesus is glorified (Jn 7:37–39). Notice in verse 37 that Jesus says;

*'If any man thirst, let him come unto **me**, and drink.'*

It does not say 'My Father' or 'The Holy Spirit'.

The question may be asked 'Does the minister baptise the candidate in the Holy Spirit when he lays hands on him according to the Scriptures?' The scriptural answer to this fair question is no. We can see from Galatians 3:5 that the minister simply acts as an instrument to minister the Spirit through the laying on of hands. The same is true of healing or deliverance. We are simply used of God for Jesus to heal or deliver with the aid of the third Person in the Trinity – namely the Holy Spirit.

Another question may be asked and often is, 'Does a person receive the baptism in the Holy Ghost at conversion?' The answer is no, and we will deal with it later. However, at this stage, it is worth noting that Hebrews 6:2 reveals a plurality of baptisms. In fact there are three baptisms revealed in the Bible. One baptism takes place at conversion and is the baptism in the likeness of

Christ's death (Rom 6:5; 1 Cor 12:13). The second is water baptism (Acts 8:38; 16:14–15) and the third, baptism in the Holy Spirit.

The opening chapter of the Acts of the Apostles once again shows that it is Jesus who, right at the very beginning of the prophesied outpouring of the Holy Spirit makes trembling, fearful Christians into Spirit-filled warriors who stand up to everything including death itself (Acts 1:3–5). Also, we see that Jesus is definitely removed from the scene before the first Christians are baptised (Acts 1:11) and this baptism in the Holy Ghost will surely continue until Jesus returns and the Holy Ghost is removed from the earth (2 Thess 2:7). As Tom Walker puts it:

> 'Can churches be satisfied to be dead, organisation-ridden, cold, lifeless, when Christ is the Baptiser in the Holy Ghost and fire?'

The Baptism with Fire

The Greek word for baptism is *'baptisma'*, which simply means baptism consisting of the processes of immersion, submersion and emergence. From this definition we conclude that total immersion into something is definitely emphasised. With the three baptisms already mentioned we can see from this definition why this word is used. Firstly, with conversion we are totally immersed and identified into Christ's death (Rom 6:3–4) then with water baptism we are totally immersed into water giving an outward testimony that the inward change has already taken place (Mt 3:13–15) and thirdly, with the baptism in the Holy Ghost, the person is totally immersed in the Holy Spirit from head to foot which is perhaps the reason why the sceptics in Jerusalem thought that the disciples were drunk (Acts 2:13) when they heard and saw the outward evidence of the Spirit-filled believers (Acts 2:6, 33; Eph 5:18–20).

When this supernatural immersion takes place our bodies are quickened (Rom 8:11) and they become temples of the Holy Spirit (1 Cor 3:16; 6:19), which is probably the reason why the Holy Ghost uses both physical and mental faculties when distributing and operating the subsequent gifts of the Holy Spirit (1 Cor 12:8–10).

In two of the Gospels we are told that fire accompanies this baptism:

> *'He shall baptize you with the Holy Ghost and with fire.'*
> (Mt 3:11)

John the Baptist goes on to say in the next verse:

> *'Whose fan is in his hand and he will throughly purge his floor, and gather his wheat into the garner, but he will burn up the chaff with unquenchable fire.'*

Consequently, we see that the fire that accompanies this baptism is a purifier to burn away all unrighteousness and iniquity. In fact the Greek word for fire is where the English word purify comes from. The Bible reveals that fire is going to *'try every man's work of what sort it is'* at the bema seat of Christ (1 Cor 3:12–15; Rev 11:18). The object of this fire is to produce Christians who will have all of their worthless deeds burned up on earth so that they may be presented faultless (Jude 24) and without blemish (Eph 5:27) at Christ's coming.

Another aspect of this fire is to produce zeal in the Christians, as the writer to the Hebrews says:

> *'Who maketh his angels spirits, and his ministers a flame of fire.'*
> (Heb 1:7)

This fire had obviously produced the desired zeal in the Corinthian believers who provoked many by their zeal (2 Cor 9:2).

Signs Following

After the great commission given in the gospel according to Mark we have the following glorious statement by Christ Himself:

> *'And these signs shall follow them that believe; in my name shall they cast out devils; they shall speak with new tongues; They shall take up serpents; and if they drink any deadly thing, it shall not hurt them; they shall lay hands on the sick, and they shall recover. And they went forth, and preached every where, the Lord working with them, and confirming the word with signs following. Amen.'* (Mk 16:17, 18, 20)

However, what is the initial sign that a believer has received the baptism in the Holy Ghost? This is revealed very clearly in the Acts of the Apostles. Even though all kinds of miraculous healings, miracles and deliverances take place throughout the Book of Acts, it definitely shows that the initial sign is speaking in tongues. This is apparent at the very beginning:

> *'And when the day of Pentecost was fully come, they were all with one accord in one place. And suddenly there came a sound from heaven as of a rushing mighty wind, and it filled all the house where they were sitting. And there appeared unto them cloven tongues like as of fire, and it sat upon each of them. And they were all filled with the Holy Ghost, and began to speak with other tongues, as the Spirit gave them utterance.'* (Acts 2:1–4)

45

This continues throughout the entire early church account, not only with Jews but Gentiles also (Acts 10:45–46), in Caesarea and again at Ephesus (Acts 19:6) with speaking in tongues closely followed by the gift of prophecy.

At this stage it should be mentioned that the speaking with tongues received at the baptism in the Spirit is different to the gift of the Spirit *'divers kinds of tongues.'* One of the easiest ways to establish this is that tongues are for personal edification and can be used at any time (1 Cor 14:4; Jude 20) whereas all of the nine gifts of the Spirit are operated *'as the Spirit wills'* (1 Cor 12:11).

There have been people who say that Paul the apostle did not speak with tongues when He received his personal baptism in the Holy Ghost (Acts 9:17–20) since it does not mention tongues. However, we may firstly state that Paul did speak in tongues (1 Cor 14:6, 18) and secondly that Paul had certainly received power to speak the word of God boldly (Acts 9:20, 22) which only comes after the baptism in the Spirit (Acts 1:8). We see further proof of this when Paul is writing to Timothy:

> *'Wherefore I put thee in remembrance, that thou stir up the gift of God, which is in thee by the putting on of my hands. For God hath not given us the Spirit of fear; but of power, and of love, and of a sound mind.'*
> (2 Tim 1:6–7)

Here we see that the power came by stirring up the gift which can only mean tongues. Thus, it is clear that Paul must have spoken in tongues when he was baptised in the Holy Ghost.

Now that we have established that speaking in tongues is the only initial evidence of the baptism in the Holy Ghost, we can now proceed to other signs and wonders that are available only after the baptism in the Spirit. In the book of Hebrews we have the comprehensive statement:

> *'God also bearing them witness, both with signs and wonders, and with divers miracles, and gifts of the Holy Ghost, according to His own will.'* (Heb 2:4)

These resultant supernatural phenomena are really the fulfilment of Jesus' words:

> *'... the works that I do shall he do also and **greater works than these shall he do**.'* (Jn 14:12)

These are seen in a manifold way throughout the Acts of the Apostles and by countless Christians today. The Acts of the Apostles itself reveals cripples healed (Acts 3:6) angelic visitation followed by deliverance (Acts 12:1–11), a man impotent from birth healed (Acts 14:8–10) as well as Paul being raised from the dead after stoning (Acts 14:9–20) and no harm coming to him after being bitten by a venomous snake (Acts 28:3–6). Today we hear of similar instances; cancers are healed, the blind, lame and paralysed are healed, people are raised from the dead, teeth are filled, wombs opened, winds change direction etc. These are all the accompanying signs along with many others to confirm the written Word of God and to convince people that Jesus is alive.

The Promise

In examining the doctrine of the baptism in the Holy Spirit we can see how the eternal triune Godhead works together. We have already seen that Jesus is the one who baptizes with the Holy Ghost which reveals the second and third persons of the trinity. Also, we see that the

Father is the one who promises this baptism to the church:

> *'And, behold, I send the promise of my Father upon you: but tarry ye in the city of Jerusalem, until ye be endued with power from on high.'*　　(Lk 24:49)

We can see that the baptism in the Holy Ghost was and is no accident but has been carefully planned and predestined for the church (Jn 14:16, 26; Acts 1:4). In the light of this fact we must be ever careful to give this promise its rightful place and indeed encourage everyone to seek and claim this promise for the edifying of the body and the resultant power to demonstrate to the world that Jesus Christ is Lord (Phil 2:11). In fact, this promise from the Father is found in Old Testament prophecy in both Joel (2:28) and Isaiah (32:15).

For Every Believer

We read in Paul's first epistle to Timothy that God wants all men to be saved (1 Tim 2:4; 2 Pet 3:9). We also read in Scripture that God is no respecter of persons (Deut 10:17; Acts 10:34; Rom 2:11; Gal 2:6; Col 3:25), a statement which is repeated and made known throughout Scripture. In the same way that God desires everyone to receive Christ as Saviour, He wants to equip everyone to serve Him with boldness. Every part of man's redemption, forgiveness, healing, deliverance, provision, sanctification and the baptism in the Holy Spirit are all for the whole church. In fact, we find that it is a commandment to be filled with the Spirit (Eph 5:18) and all God's commands are to the entire church and are not grievous (1 Jn 5:2–3). In the light of these facts alone we could honestly say that God indeed wants every believer baptised in the Holy Ghost.

48

Let us now prove directly that the baptism in the Holy Spirit is for everybody. Right at the beginning of the Holy Spirit's initial outpouring on the Day of Pentecost itself we have the conclusive statement given by Peter:

> *'Repent, and be baptised every one of you, in the name of Jesus Christ for the remission of sins, and ye shall receive the gift of the Holy Ghost. For the promise is unto you, and to your children, and **to all** that are afar off, even as many as the Lord our God shall call.'*
>
> (Acts 2:38–39)

Notice that this verse says **all**; not most or a large majority, but **all**. Paul also, in giving his discourse on the gifts of the Spirit when referring to the tongues received at the baptism in the Spirit, says *'I would that ye **all** spake with tongues'* (1 Cor 14:5a).

Also the one hundred and twenty disciples *'were all filled with the Holy Ghost, and began to speak with other tongues, as the Spirit gave them utterance'* (Acts 2:4).

Consequently, the Bible leaves no doubt whatsoever concerning the fact that everybody who has been regenerated or born-again may receive this baptism with signs following to the strengthening of the believer and the glorifying of God.

Subsequent to Salvation

Whenever a subject is followed throughout the Scriptures it will always be consistent. The subject of the baptism in the Holy Ghost is no exception. The Bible reveals that it is most definitely separate and subsequent to conversion.

If we begin with John's gospel, before the Holy Spirit was given, we find this definitive truth when Christ is teaching regarding the forthcoming third person of the Trinity:

*'He that believeth on me, as the Scripture hath said,
out of his belly shall flow rivers of living water. (But
this spake He of the Spirit, which they that believe on
Him should receive: for the Holy Ghost was not yet
given; because that Jesus was not yet glorified).'*

(Jn 7:38–39)

From this we see that it is definitely for believers and
not for unbelievers. Later on in the book we find Jesus
expounding this truth by saying:

'The Spirit of truth; whom the world cannot receive,'

and going on to say:

'For He dwelleth with you and shall be in you.'

(Jn 14:17)

The first book of Corinthians confirms this by re-
iterating this truth:

*'The natural man receiveth not the things of the Spirit
of God.'*   (1 Cor 2:14a)

The obvious place to search for any light on this
particular subject must surely be the Acts of the
Apostles. The search ends speedily because it is full of
evidence to support the stated doctrine. In the eighth
chapter we read of Philip's preaching of the gospel in
Samaria and many people accepting Christ as their
Saviour. These are then baptised in water. We then read
that the apostles Peter and John come and lay their
hands on the new converts and they are baptised in the
Holy Ghost. At the time of Saul's conversion we see that
he receives the Holy Ghost three days after his conversion (Acts 9:3–17). In the next chapter we find Peter

preaching to Cornelius and his brethren at Caesarea and very soon these Christians are baptised in the Holy Ghost as at the beginning with the initial evidence of tongues (Acts 10:31–46). In Achaia we have another group of Christians who have *'believed through grace'* (Acts 18:27) and shortly after are asked the question:

> *'Have ye received the Holy Ghost **since ye believed?** And they said unto him, we have not so much as heard whether there be any Holy Ghost.'* (Acts 19:2)

This verse proves absolutely that Paul takes it for granted that there needs to be a time between conversion and receiving the Holy Ghost (however, there need not be much time span at all as we shall see later; it shows here that it was ignorance of the baptism in the Holy Ghost that caused the delay).

In looking at all these instances throughout the Acts of the Apostles we see that there is always a gap between conversion and the baptism in the Holy Ghost and that there cannot be any confusion as to whether or not they are the same thing.

Conditional

The Bible makes it abundantly clear that although the Holy Spirit is a gift (Acts 2:38; 10:45) there are certain things that must be done first. The first thing is that we are to ask:

> *'Ask and it shall be given you ... how much more shall your heavenly Father give the Holy Spirit to them that ask Him.'* (Lk 11:9–13)

This portion of the Bible also reveals a most important feature concerning the baptism in the Spirit. It is that

51

God will only give a good gift unto His children so that there is never any worry for a candidate who is seeking to ever think that they will receive anything else from the giver of good and perfect gifts (Jas 1:17). Whenever we ask anything from God it has to be enjoined with faith (Mk 11:22–24; Heb 11:1, 6; 1 Jn 5:14–15) like the example of asking for wisdom in the book of James; *'But let him ask in faith, nothing wavering'* (Jas 1:5–6). This leads really to the next step in receiving the promise of the Spirit. That is that God gives the Holy Ghost to them that believe Him. This is made abundantly clear in the third chapter of Galatians:

> *'That we might receive the promise of the Spirit through faith.'*   (Gal 3:14b, also verses 2–3, 5–7)

This second condition should really come naturally to the believer since *'the just shall live by faith'* (Rom 1:17) and *'without faith it is impossible to please Him'* (Heb 11:6).

Thirdly, we find that obedience is most important and something to which meticulous adherence must be made (1 Sam 15:22; Mt 7:21; Jas 1:22). This is most apparent with regard to a person receiving the Holy Ghost because: *'God hath given (the Holy Ghost) to them that obey Him'* (Acts 5:32). A.R.T. Whittall says:

> 'We do not buy the favour of the Baptiser through obedience, for the Holy Ghost is given as a free unmerited gift, but, the Spirit of holiness is not attracted to take up residence in an unholy, disobedient vessel. The Spirit is attracted to a holy, obedient life as iron filings are attracted to a magnet. Many seekers have received only after they have put wrongs right with God and, where necessary with their fellow men.'

This is confirmed in a wonderful way by the following verse:

> *'For the eyes of the LORD run to and fro throughout the whole earth, to show Himself strong in the behalf of them whose heart is perfect toward Him.'*
>
> (2 Chron 16:9)

After Receiving – (Doctrine and Experience)

There are one or two points worth mentioning with regard to the actual experience of receiving the Holy Ghost. The first point is that the person who is baptised with the Spirit does the speaking in the new language. The Bible does not say that the Holy Spirit did the speaking but the people themselves (Mk 16:17; Acts 2:4; 10:46; 19:6). This has caused many people to have a lot of unnecessary travail. Another point worth noting is that *'they began to speak in tongues'* (Acts 2:4). It does not say 'they spoke a whole new language'. People are probably expecting to speak as fluently as those who have been baptised in the Spirit for a long time. The best way to view this is to think of a baby who just begins to talk. There is hesitancy and uncertainty with the first few words but then, after a while, it gains more confidence and the vocabulary builds up. So it is with the unknown tongue. One is given one or two words at first and after continual use confidence is gained and words are added.

Shortly after a person has received and begun to speak in tongues he will realise some supernatural changes in his whole spiritual life have taken place. Firstly, a realisation of power (Lk 24:49), especially in witnessing for Jesus, will be evident (Acts 1:8). Also, joy will take a giant leap ahead which will be noticed by those around. Also, there is a thirst for more of God's Word. The person will usually begin to have more of an awareness of the second coming of Christ. There will normally be a greater love for both the Saviour and for lost souls and consequently the heart will become larger and softer.

Finally, the Bible reveals several ways in which speaking in tongues will help us in every department of our spiritual lives. Firstly, tongues are for edifying our own spirits or building ourselves up (1 Cor 14:4). Secondly, praying in tongues will help in our prayer life and keep us in line with God's will (Rom 8:26; Eph 6:18). Thirdly, praying in tongues is one of the instruments that God has given to build up and bring our faith to maturity (Jude 20). Fourthly, one of the things that we cannot do enough of is give thanks. The Bible shows that we should be continually praising, worshipping and giving thanks in all things and in all circumstances (Ps 34:1; 1 Thess 5:16–18; Heb 13:15). By experience people before long, usually realise that praising in their known language is not sufficient. This is where speaking in tongues is really helpful because it seems a never-ending way of giving thanks (1 Cor 14:15–17). Even those people who have been baptised in the Holy Spirit a long time still say that the Spirit adds words to their vocabulary in the unknown tongue. Finally, the Bible tells us that the mouth is something of a problem as far as talking is concerned (Prov 10:19; 17:27–28). The Word says that *'the tongue can no man tame; it is an unruly evil, full of deadly poison'* (Jas 3:8). By constant use of the unknown tongue and with the Holy Spirit's help people are then able to fulfil the admonition given in the first chapter of James:

> *'Wherefore, my beloved brethren, let every man be swift to hear, slow to speak, slow to wrath.'*
>
> (Jas 1:19)

Conclusion

Having looked carefully at the scriptural evidence and the experience of people in Scripture and the present day, there can be no doubt whatsoever that the baptism in the Holy Ghost is absolutely essential for the church in every age. Without this wonderful experience there can be no power, or complete faith, or guidance with the aid of the gifts of the Spirit. There can also be no preaching under the anointing of the Holy Spirit to lead assemblies into God's will. Consequently, this precious baptism must always be one of the major doctrines of the church of Jesus Christ until *'that which is perfect is come'* (1 Cor 13:10).

Chapter 5

Spiritual Fruit

Introduction

The only people who can bear spiritual fruit are genuine believers in Christ Jesus. Firstly we must define what a believer on the Lord Jesus is. This is not somebody who merely believes that God exists, because Satan believes this and is predestined for the lake of fire (Jas 2:19). A believer on the Lord Jesus is someone who has admitted to God that he is a sinner and been willing to renounce and turn away from sin and receive Christ into his heart by faith, making Him his Lord and personal Saviour (Lk 18:13; 2 Tim 2:19; Acts 3:19; Gal 2:16, 20; Eph 2:13).

Once a person has turned to Christ like this he is born again (Jn 3:3; 1 Pet 1:23) and will produce fruit depending on how he develops as a Christian.

The Bible way of bearing fruit is abiding in Christ;

> *'Abide in me and I in you. As the branch cannot bear fruit of itself, except it abide in the vine; no more can ye, except ye abide in me. I am the vine, ye are the branches: He that abideth in me, and I in him, the same bringeth forth much fruit: for without me ye can do nothing.'* (Jn 15:4–5)

The Greek for abide is *'meno'*. It can mean stay (Is 26:3), continue (Jn 15:9), dwell (Rom 8:9), endure (Mt 24:13), remain (1 Jn 2:24), stand (Eph 6:11, 13), or tarry for or wait for (1 Cor 1:7). The way to abide is by continuing in His commandments and doing those things that are pleasing in His sight (1 Jn 3:22).

> *'And hereby we do know that we know Him, if we keep His commandments. He that saith I know Him, and keepeth not His commandments is a liar and the truth is not in him. But whoso keepeth His Word, in him verily is the love of God perfected: hereby know we that we are in Him. He that saith he abideth in Him ought himself also so to walk, even as He walked.'*
>
> (1 Jn 2:3–6)

The Word of God also tells us of the paramount importance of love:

> *'Herein is my Father glorified, that ye bear much fruit; so shall ye be my disciples. If ye keep my commandments, ye shall abide in my love; even as I have kept my Father's commandments, and abide in His love. This is my commandment that ye love one another as I have loved you.'* (Jn 15:8, 10, 12)

Unlike the gifts of the Spirit, which are distributed to each man severally (1 Cor 12:11) as the Spirit wills, the fruit of the Spirit is a cluster of virtues which hang together and ideally are indivisible. Just as white light is produced by the blending of the seven primary colours, so the true righteousness of the saints is the product of the blending of these nine virtues (2 Pet 1:5–8). The Christian is likened unto a tree (Ps 1:3). This tree is given nine seeds at regeneration. As this tree is watered these seeds grow and help the others to grow. At the beginning the fruit is not obvious but with time it buds and eventually the fruit appears in the Christian. The end product is righteousness, holiness and godliness which brings much pleasure to the gardener who does all the pruning.

The fruit is the product of the Spirit of Christ;

> '... *being filled with the fruits of righteousness, which are by Jesus Christ, unto the glory and praise of God.*'
> (Phil 1:11)

It is the outcome of the regenerated life (Tit 3:5), and is produced by the Spirit of Christ who dwells within believers.

The Nine-Fold Fruit of the Spirit (Gal 5:22–23)

Love – (agape)

This word love is a purely biblical and ecclesiastical word and denotes affection, good-will, love, benevolence (Jn 15:13; Rom 13:10; 1 Jn 4:18). The number of times it occurs in the Bible, particularly in the Pauline epistles and the writings of John, demonstrate the absolute importance of love in every department of the Christian's life and walk with God.

> '*A new commandment I give unto you, that ye love one another; as I have loved you, that ye also love one another. By this shall all men know that ye are my disciples, if ye have love one to another.*'
> (Jn 13:34–35)

In the New Testament agape is used to denote the highest form of love. The believer experiences the very nature of God at the new birth which is love itself (1 Jn 4:16). As John Lancaster puts it:

'Love is the motive force behind his new attitude to life.' (2 Cor 5:14)

The kind of love that God instills in His new creations enables them to love the unlovely (Mt 5:43–48) and to show compassion and a deep concern all the time (1 Cor 13:4–8a). When a Christian is leading a totally yielded life, walking in the Spirit and experiencing victory (Rom 6:19; Gal 5:16, 25; 1 Jn 5:1–4), he is able to love as he is transformed by the renewing of his mind (Rom 12:2). He grows in grace and in the knowledge of the Saviour Jesus Christ (2 Pet 3:18), and as he experiences and manifests the precious promises in the Word he will be able to love more because he will become more like the divine nature every day (2 Pet 1:4). Hallelujah! If God be for us, who can be against us?

We serve a God of love (2 Cor 13:11) who is the source of all true love (1 Jn 4:7). We experience the love of God in and through our lives (Rom 5:5) in an overflowing way. God gives to us a spirit of love (2 Tim 1:7) which is enjoined with power and a sound mind. His love is a continual comfort to us that we may comfort others (Phil 2:1; 2 Cor 1:3–4).

In conclusion, we can say that Christians should show and demonstrate all the qualities of love to others that God shows to us. Here is the picture taken from one of F.E. Marsh's books, who shows the character of the love of God as manifested in Christ, and shows what should be the character of our love to Him;

1. His suffering love. *'Love suffereth long'* (Lk 22:44).
2. His compassionate love. *'Is kind'* (Lk 10:33).
3. His contented love. *'Envieth not'* (Lk 22:42).
4. His self-abasing love. *'Vaunteth not itself'* (Jn 4:34).
5. His humbling love. *'Not puffed up'* (Phil 2:7, 8).
6. His wise love. *'Doth not behave unseemly'* (Jn 7:46).
7. His unselfish love. *'Seeketh not her own'* (Jn 17:22).

8. His patient love. *'Not easily provoked'* (Jn 21:15–17).
9. His unsuspicious love. *'Thinketh no evil'* (Lk 7:39).
10. His holy love. *'Rejoiceth not in iniquity'* (Jn 2:15).
11. His truthful love. *'Rejoiceth in the truth'* (Lk 24:26).
12. His bearing love. *'Beareth all things'* (Gen 45:1).
13. His expecting love. *'Hopeth all things'* (Acts 7:56).
14. His trusting love. *'Believeth all things'* (Jn 17:18).
15. His enduring love. *'Endureth all things'* (Heb 12:2).
16. His unchanging love. *'Never faileth'* (Jn 13:1).

All these qualities in the Saviour, and many more, sum up what this fruit really is. Paul expresses his desire for Christians like this:

> *'I pray that your love may abound yet more and more in knowledge and in all judgement.'* (Phil 1:9)

> *'The Lord direct your hearts into the love of God, and into the patient waiting for Christ.'* (2 Thess 3:5)

Joy – (chara)

The Greek word means cheerfulness, exceedingly joyful, greatly glad. This is what the Christian should experience most of the time. The fruit of joy is a radiant testimony for Jesus. The Word says; *'The joy of the Lord is your strength'* (Neh 8:10); and, *'In thy presence is fulness of joy'* (Ps 16:11). It also says *'Ye rejoice with joy unspeakable* (to which words are inadequate) *and full of glory'* (1 Pet 1:8). As we are filled with all the fullness of God (Eph 3:19) our joy will increase and know no bounds.

Christian joy has God as its author (Phil 4:4). This fruit grows in all circumstances as the Scriptures make absolutely plain (2 Cor 6:10; 7:4; 1 Pet 1:6–8; Jas 1:2), particularly when trials come. This is when the Christian has to learn to rejoice always (Heb 13:15; 1 Thess 5:16) and not to rely on feelings but faith (2 Cor 1:24).

This joy comes from God through His Word and the Holy Spirit (1 Thess 1:6; Rom 14:17; 15:13; Ps 119:1, 14, 111, 162). Our joy is strengthened through the mutual fellowship of our brothers and sisters in Christ (Rom 12:15; 2 Cor 2:3; Phil 2:2, 17), and will only be full by abiding in Christ (Jn 15:11).

The Bible says that we *'rejoice in hope of the glory of God'* (Rom 5:2). The joy also anticipates eschatalogically the joy of being with Christ forever (Tit 2:13; Rom 12:12; Rev 19:7).

Peace – (eirene)

This word means quietness, rest, set at one again, unity or concord. The fruit of peace is calmness of soul. One person has said about this peace;

> 'it is the tranquil state of a soul assured of its Salvation through Christ, and so fearing nothing from God and content with its earthly lot, of whatsoever sort it is.'

Paul says; *'to be spiritually minded is life and peace'* (Rom 8:6). The kind of peace that the world cannot give (Jn 14:27; 16:33) is only found through knowing the author of peace (1 Cor 14:33). Paul goes on to say that the prayerful life will promote God's peace (Phil 4:6–7). He also tells us to *'follow after the things which make for peace'* (Rom 14:19).

The kind of peace that the Christian experiences is very powerful because, like joy, it is not dependent upon our circumstances whatsoever. Believers experience peace in their minds because they are absolutely sure of going to heaven (Rom 5:1; Eph 2:14–17; Col 1:20).

The Bible says; *'Thou wilt keep him in perfect peace whose mind is stayed on Thee'* (Is 26:3) which is so true in our experience as we continue in obedience to His commandments (Lev 26:3–6). To be complete in Christ (Col 2:10) is to have a complete peace, because we are in a complete Saviour.

When the peace of God rules in the heart (Col 3:15), through being anxious for nothing, then in the calmness and quietness which are begotten by the Holy Ghost (Rom 15:13) the life shall be calm as a river (Is 66:12), and the peace of God will beam from us like *'an angel'* (Acts 6:15).

Longsuffering – *(makrothumia)*

The Greek can be translated as patience, endurance, constancy, steadfastness, perseverance, slowness in avenging wrongs. The fruit of longsuffering is the repentance and salvation in others (Rom 2:4; 1 Tim 1:16; 2 Tim 3:10; 4:2); *'And account that the longsuffering of our Lord is salvation'* (2 Pet 3:15a).

The Bible exhorts us to be longsuffering in our dealings with fellow believers (Eph 4:2; 1 Thess 5:14) and tells us *'love suffereth long'* (1 Cor 13:4). It is usually easy to be patient when everything is alright but the test comes when things go wrong. This is the time when the Christian should stand out in the crowd and demonstrate the major virtue of longsuffering (1 Pet 2:20; 2 Cor 6:4–6; Heb 6:12) which will lead to the Salvation of precious souls (Gal 6:9; Jas 5:7).

The Oxford Dictionary defines longsuffering as the suffering or enduring (of pain, trouble, or evil) with calmness and composure. It is forbearance under provocation of any kind especially bearing with others with their faults and limitations.

Throughout the Bible God demonstrates His longsuffering with sinful man (Ex 34:6; Neh 9:6–38, especially verses 15–17; Joel 2:13) and since we are to be partakers of the divine nature (2 Pet 1:4) longsuffering should be a major characteristic in believers (Prov 14:29; 15:18; 16:32).

Gentleness – (chrestotes)

This word means moral goodness, integrity and kindness. The dictionary describes gentleness as courtesy, politeness, mildness and freedom from harshness or violence. The fruit of gentleness is yielding (2 Cor 10:1) and being gracious (1 Pet 2:3).

The word *'chrestotes'* is translated also as kindness (2 Cor 6:6; Eph 2:7; Col 3:12; Tit 3:4) in the Bible. Kindnesses, says J.R. Miller, are

> 'the small coins of love. We should always be ready to scatter these bright coins wherever we go. Kindnesses are usually little things that we do as we go along the way.'

We never know what kind of blessing we may bestow upon someone with a gentle word in the love of Christ. Kindness is God-like in its action and proves we know His love to us. Kindness is an obligation of our faith for we are exhorted to *'Be kindly affectioned one to another with brotherly love'* or kindness (Rom 12:10; Heb 13:1).

God's character is gentle and yet powerful. Only in Christ can we possibly achieve this for ourselves (Tit 3:1–2). Jesus demonstrated gentleness in His earthly ministry when so often He put to silence His enemies, and also with His dealing with His disciples and sinners.

Goodness – (agathosune)

The Greek word *'agathosune'* is found only in biblical and ecclesiastical writings. It means uprightness of heart and life (2 Thess 1:11; Eph 5:9) and beneficence. The Oxford Dictionary tells us that goodness means being morally excellent, holy, kind, agreeable, amusing, wholesome, favourable, useful, reliable for a purpose, efficient; and beneficence means doing good, active kindness i.e. an act that is beneficial to others. All these qualities are produced by the Christian who is moving on with God.

God is essentially and absolutely good (Mt 19:17; Mk 10:18; Lk 18:19). The mercy and virtue of God's goodness leads man to repentance (Rom 2:4; 11:22). Christians are to prove His goodness (Rom 12:2) cleave to it (Rom 12:9), to do that which is good (Rom 2:10; Gal 6:10; 1 Pet 3:11; Jn 5:29), to work it (Rom 2:10; Eph 4:28; 6:8) to follow after it (1 Thess 5:15) to be zealous of it (1 Pet 3:13), to imitate it (3 Jn 11), to overcome evil with it (Rom 12:21), and to be filled with it (Rom 15:14). One writer said;

> 'The goodness that the Spirit produces is not the frigid sterility of a moral iceberg, but the mellow fruitfulness of a life ripened by the sun of righteousness.'

Faith – (pistis)

James Strong translates *'pistis'* as a reliance (upon Christ for salvation) and constancy (in such profession), assurance, belief, faith and fidelity. The fruit of faith is faithfulness. As Barclay put it;

> 'Faith in God and His Word is the basis of our relationship with Him and the avenue through which His blessings flow into our lives.'

The Bible gives us many verses on the subject of faith. It gives us a clear definition of what it is (Heb 11:1), how to use it (Mk 11:22–24), where it comes from (Rom 4:17) and where to look for it (2 Cor 4:18; Col 3:1–2).

Real faith is complete trust in God's Word. As the

Bible is read (Rom 10:17) and acted upon (Jas 1:22), a Christian will use less and less sense-knowledge faith (faith which believes only when we can see, hear, touch, taste or smell what was asked for), and more and more real faith which believes God without any evidence. This faith is not just for our initial conversion but throughout our entire life. As we walk with Him, faith should become 'second nature' to us; we should use real faith without hardly thinking about it in our prayers (1 Jn 3:22; 5:14–15; Phil 4:6).

Faith should grow daily as we give diligence to it (2 Pet 1:5) and as we build up ourselves in tongues (Jude 20; 1 Cor 14:4). As we act on God's Word for everything (2 Tim 3:16–17; Heb 4:12), we shall stand by faith (2 Cor 1:24b).

Meekness – (praotes)

The word *'praotes'* can be translated humility, meekness, mild or humble. The Oxford Dictionary tells us that meek means submissive or gentle, and humble means having or showing a low estimate of one's own importance, lowly and modest.

In the Bible the meaning of meekness is certainly not a weak or cowardly quality. On the contrary Christ calls Himself meek (Mt 11:29; 21:5), and Paul refers to our Saviour as being meek and gentle (2 Cor 10:1). Also we see that meekness is not just outward but rather an inwrought grace of the soul, and the exercising of it is first and chiefly towards God (Jas 4:10).

Believers are to show meekness to all men (Tit 3:2) because it is an attribute of His chosen ones (Col 3:12). Paul exhorts Timothy to *'follow after meekness'* (1 Tim 6:11) and also talks about believers exhibiting a *'spirit of meekness'* (1 Cor 4:21; Gal 6:1). In the task of correcting people, Christians are to show meekness (2 Tim 2:25) to those who *'oppose themselves.'* The born-again Christian is to *'receive with meekness the engrafted word'* (Jas 1:21), he is to *'seek meekness'* (Zeph 2:3). The women are to bear a *'meek and quiet spirit'* to their husbands (1 Pet 3:1–4). We are to share our faith with meekness and fear (1 Pet 3:15).

The Lord gives a series of promises to those who are meek:

- *'the meek shall eat and be satisfied'* (Ps 22:26);
- *'the meek shall inherit the earth and have peace'* (Ps 37:11);
- *'The Lord lifteth up the meek'* (Ps 147:6);
- 'The meek also shall increase their joy in the Lord' (Is 29:19).

Meekness is the Queen of Graces. It does not seek the throne of importance. Humility walks consistently, loves generously, serves willingly, acts meekly, forgives heartily, forbears thoughtfully and responds obediently. Peter says;

> *'For God resisteth the proud, and giveth grace to the humble. Humble yourselves therefore under the mighty hand of God, that He may exalt you in due time.'*   (1 Pet 5:5–6)

We can only experience the power of God working for us when we are under the *'mighty hand of God.'*

Temperance – *(enkrateia)*

The Greek word means self-control or more fully, the virtue of one who masters his desires and passions, especially his sensual appetites. The fruit that is produced by temperance is patience (2 Pet 1:6), spiritual and physical health (1 Cor 9:24–27), and the ability to contain and to have inward self-control and power over the passions (1 Cor 7:9).

The Bible gives us a few examples of temperance. Paul

in sharing his faith with Felix (Acts 24:24–25); Daniel with regard to food (Dan 1:8); Joseph in fighting against his personal feelings (Gen 43:30, 31); and the Lord Jesus, since neither popularity (Jn 6:15), suffering (Lk 22:42–44) or personal insults (1 Pet 2:23) could provoke Jesus from consistently demonstrating a self-controlled, self-disciplined and calm disposition (1 Cor 9:25). W.E. Vine says of temperance;

> 'The various powers bestowed by God upon man are capable of abuse, the right use demands the controlling power of the will under the operation of the Spirit of God.'

Conclusion

Although the list of nine fruits (Gal 5:22–23) gives us an example of a well-ordered Christian life it is not exhaustive. There are at least six other fruits of the Spirit mentioned in the Scriptures. There is holiness, which is separation from *'all that is in the world'* (1 Jn 2:16). The fruit of holiness is the ability to be used of God (Rom 6:22). This verse of Scripture gives us another fruit; everlasting life. The fruit of everlasting life is heavenly citizenship (Gal 6:8; Jn 6:39). Liberality or generosity is another virtue (Rom 15:28; 2 Cor 8:2; 1 Cor 16:3), the fruit of which is blessing (Acts 20:35), soul pleasure and reward (Lk 14:13–14). Righteousness or justice is also mentioned in Scripture, which has as its fruit grace and good works (2 Cor 9:8–10; Jas 3:18; Eph 5:9). Truth is also mentioned (Eph 5:9) which is our word, genuineness, honesty and sincerity. The fruit of truth is spiritual light and understanding and also to be well-informed (2 Tim 2:7; Col 1:9; 4:6). Lastly, there is heavenly wisdom which is wisdom from above (Jas 3:17). The fruit of this is:

> *'first pure, then peaceable, gentle, and easy to be intreated, full of mercy and good fruits, without partiality and without hypocrisy.'*

In conclusion Samuel Chadwick sums up the fruit of the Spirit as;

> 'An affectionate, lovable disposition, a radiant spirit and a cheerful temper, a tranquil mind and a quiet manner, a forbearing patience in provoking circumstances and with trying people, a sympathetic insight and tactful helpfulness, generous judgement and a big-souled charity, loyalty and reliableness under all circumstance, humility that forgets self in the joy of others, in all things self-mastered and self-controlled, which is the final mark of perfecting.'

We cannot bear this kind of fruit ourselves but it is His mighty power that works in and through us (Eph 1:19; 3:19, 20; Col 1:29). In fact the fruit of the Spirit is the outworking of the Holy Spirit's inworking (2 Cor 3:18). The fruit of the Spirit will blossom and grow as sanctification becomes a major priority in the lives of believers (Rom 6:19; 1 Cor 1:30; 2 Cor 9:10; 1 Thess 4:3–4).

Chapter 6

The Gifts of the Holy Spirit

Introduction

After a person has found Christ as his Lord and personal Saviour he is then scripturally required to seek for the baptism in the Holy Spirit. Then he can claim and manifest the gifts of the Holy Spirit.

The Bible tells us that we are to *'desire spiritual gifts'* (1 Cor 14:1), which shows that they must be significant in the Church of Jesus Christ. In fact we find that the apostle Paul spent three chapters explaining what these gifts are and how we should use them, so that all things may be done decently and in order (1 Cor 12:13, 14; 14:10). By a careful examination of the Scriptures we see that the baptism in the Holy Ghost and the resultant gifts of the Spirit form a very vital part in proclaiming the message of the gospel (Rom 15:19; Heb 2:4). In the gospel of Mark, Jesus teaches that;

> *'These signs shall follow them that believe; In my name shall they cast out devils; they shall speak with new tongues; They shall take up serpents; and if they drink any deadly thing, it shall not hurt them; they shall lay hands on the sick, and they shall recover.*

*And they went forth and preached everywhere, the
Lord working with them, and confirming the word
with signs following.'*   (Mk 16:17, 18, 20)

The main reason for the gifts of the Spirit is for edification or the building up of the believers (1 Cor 12:7;
14:3, 4, 5, 12, 26). The other reasons are for exhortation
and comfort for believers (1 Cor 14:3) and convicting
unbelievers of sin (1 Cor 14:22, 24). Another important
point regarding the gifts of the Spirit is that the Holy
Spirit gives the varying gifts *'as he will'* (1 Cor 12:11). In
other words believers cannot choose which gifts they are
going to receive. Ron Jones sums up the gifts as follows:

> 'The nine gifts of the Holy Spirit then, are super-
> natural equipment for witness and for worship and
> as such they have never been withdrawn.'

The nine gifts of the Holy Spirit mentioned in
1 Corinthians 12:8–10 can be put into three groups:

The gifts of revelation (to know)
- A word of Wisdom
- A word of Knowledge
- Discerning of Spirits

The gifts of power (to do)
- Faith
- Working of Miracles
- Gifts of Healings

The gifts of inspired utterance (to speak)
- Prophecy
- Divers kinds of Tongues
- Interpretation of Tongues

We will now examine each gift in the above order.

The Gifts of Revelation

A Word of Wisdom

A definition of this gift is supernatural revelation of the Divine purpose, the application of knowledge or instruction (Acts 23:17). It must be said that this gift is not natural wisdom, but supernatural wisdom. It is wisdom bestowed by the Holy Ghost and thus separate from human wisdom. It is a revelation of the mind and will of God.

The Greek text says *'logos sophias'* without the article which means a correct translation is '**a** word of wisdom' and not '**the** word of wisdom'. This is significant because when this gift is in operation God gives only a very small part of His wisdom to or through the Spirit-filled believer.

An example from Scripture is Paul's encounter on his voyage to Rome in Acts 27:1–44. All hope was gone amongst the men on the ship because of the tempest (verse 18). However, Paul was able to say with all boldness:

> *'And now I exhort you to be of good cheer; for there shall be no loss of any man's life among you, but of the ship. For there stood by me this night the angel of God, whose I am and whom I serve, saying, Fear not, Paul; thou must be brought before Caesar: and, lo, God hath given thee all them that sail with thee.'*
>
> (verses 22–24)

The last verse of chapter 27 tells us the fulfillment of this word of Wisdom; *'they escaped all safe to land.'*

This gift of the Holy Spirit is not just confined to the Early Church, or to the Church age but is apparent in the Old Covenant also. It can be said that Moses operated this gift to give the ten commandments (Deut 5:1–21), as did Elijah when he anointed Hazael (1 Kings 19:15). Jonah spoke to Nineveh by a word of Wisdom (Jon 1:2). We can say that the gift of the Spirit 'a word of Wisdom' can be manifested through the audible Divine voice, angelic visitation, by dream or vision, through other spiritual gifts such as prophecy and combined tongues and interpretation. It can even be used by a preacher under the anointing of the Holy Ghost. Through this gift God's purpose can be revealed concerning people, things, events in the future, events of nations or places.

A modern day illustration of this gift in action involves an elderly woman of God who ran a kitchen bakery. One Friday evening as she was counting her takings a voice said to her 'put that money away'. She ignored the voice since there was nobody around. The voice again said, 'put that money away', much louder. She recognised it as God's voice and acknowledged Him. The voice came much louder and she feared and hid the money under a cushion. Immediately two roughs burst through the door and demanded her money, threatening her with a pistol and holding her by the throat. She told them she was a child of God and commanded them to leave in the Name of Jesus. The two ran off. Thus the word of Wisdom from the Lord prevented her from being robbed, and most probably encouraged her faith and boldness to take authority over the attackers. Hence, as Ron Jones expresses it;

> 'A word of Wisdom may come to give warning of future danger, or to give guidance, confirmation or assurance to a person, to a church or to a movement.'

Of this we can be absolutely sure, that in every case it is a miracle and it is a manifestation of the Holy Spirit *'to profit withal'* (1 Cor 12:7).

A Word of Knowledge

The definition of a 'word of knowledge' is the super-natural revelation of facts from the mind of God to the Spirit-filled believer. This word of knowledge cannot be obtained by studying the Word or by being highly intelligent. Neither can it be obtained through education or experience in any field. The fact is that God the Holy Spirit gives it without merit. George Jeffreys tells us that;

> 'It is not the natural ability to explain or analyse, or to pursue to a logical conclusion. Neither is it a gift of knowledge, which like eternal life is given once and for all. It is the bestowal of a word of knowledge on special occasions.'

Preachers have experienced the use of this gift under the anointing of the Holy Spirit, and have often been surprised by saying things which were previously unknown to them (1 Jn 2:27). Also when studying God's precious Word the Spirit has been known to shed light on an otherwise obscure portion, by a word of knowledge.

There are several examples in the Bible where the word of knowledge is used. Peter was commanded to go with some men by a word of knowledge in Acts 10:19. Saul through a vision was given the name of Ananias (Acts 9:11, 12) and through the same gift Ananias was told to go to the street called Straight enquiring after Saul (Acts 9:11). This shows that both ministers and laymen can be used in spiritual gifts. A tremendous example of this gift in action is found in the book of Revelation where the apostle John was *'in the Spirit on the Lord's day'* and had imparted to him the situations of the seven churches in Asia while he was a prisoner on the Isle of Patmos (Rev

1:9–3:22). There was no human way of knowing what was going on at that time in all the churches but by the supernatural gift of a word of knowledge, and thus John was able to write to each respective Pastor for exhortation, rebuke, and encouragement.

A recent illustration of this gift will be helpful here. A missionary was once in a critical condition and almost at the point of death. All of a sudden he arose up to perfect health and full vigour. He discovered later that a young lady had been given a detailed description through a revelation of God's knowledge, at the very hour of the missionary's traumatic and close encounter with death. She spent some time agonizing in the unknown tongue until God gave her a vision of the missionary perfectly restored.

The word of knowledge then is a supernatural revelation to know men's thoughts (1 Sam 9:19; Acts 5:3); to recover lost property or people; to reveal the cause of sickness or demon possession or to reveal certain facts in people's lives for correction and reproof.

Discerning of Spirits

This gift is often confused with discernment. However, Scripture reveals that discernment and discerning of spirits are separate (1 Cor 2:13–15 for discernment). The definition of 'discerning of spirits' is the supernatural insight into the realm of spirits. Ron Jones says of the gift:

> 'It is not discernment of motive or character. It is not the ability to discover faults, nor is it a brand of spiritual psychological insight. It is rather the supernatural power of the Spirit enabling one to receive insight into the secret realm of spirits, and is given by the Holy Spirit to give protection to God's people against the counterfeits of the adversary.'

The days in which we are living are said to be perilous times (2 Tim 3:1), since they are most certainly the last days. We are warned in Scripture that some shall depart from the faith, giving heed to seducing spirits, and doctrines of devils (1 Tim 4:1–3). We see all around us the fulfilment of such Scriptures with the rapid increase of occultism, satanism and witchcraft, not to mention false cults and sects which have a form of godliness (2 Tim 3:5) and deny His power through the blood of Jesus Christ (Rev 12:11). Also, we remember that Satan masquerades himself as an angel of light (2 Cor 11:14) and is constantly roaming about seeking whom he may devour (1 Pet 5:8). We can see by this the very necessary operation of the discerning of spirits to free men and women from the power of the devil. It is important to note that the gift only discerns their presence and does not cast out demons. In the many cases where Jesus has to deal with demon possession and oppression it is by His word that the devils come out of their victims (Mk 5:8; 9:25; Mt 17:18).

In the Acts of the Apostles we see that Paul has to deal with a demon possessed girl (Acts 16:16–18). An interesting thing to note is that he does not deal with her immediately but waits for the operation of this gift to be manifested when the time is right (verse 18). He is then able to take authority over the demon of Puthonos (python or divination) in the mighty name of Jesus causing her deliverance without any fear of being hurt (Lk 10:19; 1 Jn 4:4; Mk 16:17).

Hence, this gift is used to help the afflicted, oppressed or tormented; to discover one who is a servant of the devil (Acts 13:9–11), or to expose error (2 Pet 2:1). It is particularly important today with so many under the power of the devil. Through these three gifts God is able to make known to His children any particular aspect of His knowledge at any given time.

The Gifts of Power

Faith

There are three types of faith mentioned in the Bible; firstly, faith to believe unto salvation (Rom 12:3; Eph 2:8); secondly, the fruit of the Spirit (Gal 5:22; 2 Pet 1:5) and finally, the gift of faith. The latter is under consideration and is the supernatural trust in God for the miraculous (1 Cor 12:9).

This gift of the Spirit is usually used in conjunction with one or more of the other gifts. For example, when Paul is used of God in Asia for *'special miracles'* (Acts 19:11–12) it would be fair to say that the gifts of miracles, healings and faith were used if not discerning of spirits also. When Jesus and the apostles raise someone from the dead by the power of God it must have taken the gift of faith and working of miracles to perform such feats (Jn 11:43; Acts 9:40). We can understand now why this gift comes under the heading of 'gifts of power' – which had tremendous results in winning the lost to Christ (Jn 11:45; Acts 9:42).

In the Bible there are cases of this gift of faith used on its own without the necessity of other gifts – which demonstrates its importance as a separate gift. When Jesus sleeps on the stormy sea He will have been endowed with supernatural faith (Mk 4:37–40) and then would have used the gift of faith combined with miracles to calm the storm. When Daniel was in the lions' den he, too, must have experienced the gift of faith to be without fear when at death's door (Dan 6:16–23).

A relatively modern example of this gift in action involves Smith Wigglesworth while raising a lady from the dead:

> 'I began to penetrate the heavens with my prayers with what faith I had. All the time my wife was

shaking me saying, "stop praying, she is already dead, it is too late." But I just kept praying. Soon I came to the end of my faith and when I did I was conscious of a faith which took hold of me that could not be denied. While I was praying in my own faith it seemed as if God said "no, no," but when this other faith came over me, I looked right up into heaven and He said, "yes, yes." The next thing I knew without intending to do it, without realizing what I was doing I got hold of that woman and pulled her out of the bed. I stood her up against the wall and commanded her to walk in Jesus' name, and she started breathing and started walking and was raised up.'

Without the supernatural gift of faith the church is lacking a significant proportion of its power but with it we can expect revival and believe for the impossible.

The Working of Miracles

Harold Horton gives a comprehensive definition of what a miracle is by saying:

'A miracle, therefore, is a supernatural intervention in the ordinary course of nature, a temporary suspension of the accustomed order; an interruption of the system of nature as we know it. The gift of the working of miracles operates by the energy or dynamic force of the Spirit in reversals or suspensions of natural laws. A miracle is a sovereign act of the Spirit of God irrespective of laws or systems.'

An obvious example of this gift is when Peter raises up Tabitha from the dead by the Spirit of God. Naturally speaking, absolutely nothing can be done for her. There has to be a reversal of natural laws for her to breathe again (Acts 9:40). Another example is when Jesus turns the water into wine at the wedding. This is done by the gift of the working of miracles to manifest forth His glory (Jn 2:1–11). In the Old Testament there are countless miracles worked through men of God such as Moses who divides the waters (Ex 14:21); strikes water from the rock (Ex 17:6); and destroys the people of Korah (Num 16:32); all achieved through this gift of the working of miracles. We can also mention Joshua with his long day (Josh 10:12–13), Samson contending with the Philistines (Judg 14:19) and when Dagon's house was pulled down (Judg 16:30). Elijah stops the rain through this gift (1 Kings 17:1; Jas 5:17), and his sacrifice is consumed with fire (1 Kings 18:38).

In the New Testament we read in Galatians:

> *'He therefore that ministereth to you the Spirit, and worketh miracles among you, doeth he it by the works of the law, or by the hearing of faith?'* **(Gal 3:5)**

Whenever a minister lays hands on believers to receive the baptism in the Holy Ghost, the working of miracles is evident (Acts 19:6). Also, when prayer is made for a person without a limb, for example, which grows to its full size, it is again in operation. We can see here the difference between the gifts of healings and the working of miracles; the example of the grown limb is beyond the scope of the gifts of healings but can only be dealt with by the working of miracles.

The gift of the working of miracles was given to confirm the Word of God (Heb 2:4; Mk 16:17–20). Miracles are still very evident throughout the world which confirms the words of Jesus in the gospel of John:

> *'Verily, verily, I say unto you, he that believeth on me, the works that I do shall he do also; and* **greater**

> **works than these shall he do**; *because I go unto my Father.'* (Jn 14:12).

Finally, as Kenneth Hagin puts it;

> 'The difference between the gift of faith and the working of miracles is that the gift of faith receives a miracle and the working of miracles works a miracle.'

The Gifts of Healings

The Greek word *'Iamaton'* is used in 1 Corinthians 12:9, 28, 30 and should be translated 'healings'. The definition of the gift (or gifts) is the supernatural power to heal diseases and infirmities without the aid of any natural means. Harold Horton says of this gift:

> 'They are the miraculous manifestation of the Spirit for the banishment of all human ills whether organic, functional or nervous, acute or chronic.'

This particular manifestation of the Spirit is used widely during the days of Jesus before the New Covenant is established. Jesus Himself operates these gifts on numerous occasions. He heals *'all manner of sickness'* and all manner of disease in Galilee (Mt 4:23), He heals a leper (Mt 8:3), He *'healed all that were sick'* (Mt 8:16). He heals a man with a withered hand (Mt 12:13); the lame, blind, dumb and maimed found their healing also by Jesus (Mt 15:30). So we see that this gift is not absent to confirm the Word in Christ's day. The disciples of Jesus are also given this gift before He dies (Mt 10:1; Mk 3:15). This gift is also promised by Jesus in the gospel of Mark to confirm the Word after Jesus returns to His Father (16:18).

After Pentecost we see the establishment of the early church which includes the gifts of healings. We read that Paul operates this gift on the Isle of Melita amongst the *'barbarous people'* (Acts 28:8–9).

We can see that one does not have to have any medical diplomas to use these gifts or any such knowledge. However, it is wrong to say that every believer has this manifestation. In fact, like all the other gifts of the Spirit, God gives these gifts of healings to whom He will and one can only use it as the Spirit leads.

The Scriptures declare that these gifts are: to deliver the sick and to destroy the devil's work in peoples' bodies; to establish Jesus's claims; to prove the gospel message; to draw people within the sound of the gospel (Jn 6:2); to turn men and women to God; to convince unbelievers of the truth of God's Word and to bring glory to God.

The Gifts of Inspired Utterance

Prophecy

Prophecy is the first of the vocal gifts. It is the supernatural utterance in the known tongue. The Word of God tells us that such prophecies are fallible and need to be judged (Greek, *discerned*, 1 Cor 14:29) by everyone present in the meeting. Thus, this supernatural gift of the Holy Spirit is different from Bible prophecy because the Bible does not need anyone to judge its infallibility (2 Pet 1:19–21). The Holy Scriptures are consequently our guidelines. For example, God would never give a prophet a prophecy which contradicted the Bible.

In 1 Corinthians 14:3 we are told what this gift is for; *'but he that prophesieth speaketh unto men to edification, and exhortation, and comfort.'* It also says that prophecy can be the means of bringing someone to Christ (1 Cor 14:24); or warning of a famine (Acts 9:28); also to warn of future persecution in the life of Paul (Acts 21:10–11).

As we read through the Scriptures we see that God has made very careful guidelines for the use of this gift so that *'all things be done decently and in order'* (1 Cor 14:40). The Word tells us that *'the spirits of the prophets are subject to the prophets'* (1 Cor 14:32) which shows God's wisdom since chaos could be caused if people started prophesying during the preaching of the Word. Hence, when the Spirit moves upon someone to prophesy, he is to wait until a convenient moment. Also, there is to be a maximum of three prophecies per meeting (1 Cor 14:29) which is wise in two directions: firstly to prevent people from going overboard and having a meeting full of prophecies, and secondly to enable people to remember the prophecies and take in what God said. In verse 31 we are clearly told to wait until someone else has finished prophesying before delivering one ourselves. Paul shows that people are to *'prophesy according to the proportion of faith'* (Rom 12:6) which shows that faith is certainly needed to prophesy. Also, Paul tells us to *'despise not prophesyings'* (1 Thess 5:20), *'desire ... that ye may prophesy'* (1 Cor 14:1) and *'covet to prophesy'* (1 Cor 14:39) which exemplifies the importance of this gift in the church of Jesus Christ.

In the exhortation of Paul to Timothy we see that God uses the gift of prophecy with the laying on of hands to impart to Timothy a gift of the Spirit to equip him for the ministry (1 Tim 4:14). This demonstrates that occasionally personal prophecies can be given directly to a person but this is the exception rather than the rule in Scripture, since the main teaching on the gift of prophecy shows the use of it to the assembly as a whole (1 Cor 14:5, 12, 19, 23).

Divers Kinds of Tongues

This gift of the Holy Spirit is defined as the supernatural utterance in an unknown tongue or language. Unknown, that is, to the speaker. This gift of the Spirit is often confused with the tongue that a person receives at his or her baptism in the holy Ghost. The Bible reveals that they are separate. A person that has been baptised in the Holy Ghost may use his supernaturally endowed language anytime he wants to for the sake of edifying himself and praising God. Paul exhorted Timothy to stir up his tongues to keep his fire burning brightly (2 Tim 1:6–7). Thus, tongues can be used anytime. However, this is not the case with the nine gifts of the Holy Ghost. A person who has the gifts of healings cannot go around every hospital laying hands on the sick at his own will for instance; or someone with the gift of prophecy cannot prophesy at will. No, rather, the gifts of the Spirit are given by the Spirit as He wills (1 Cor 12:11).

A further difference between tongues and divers kinds of tongues is that tongues need no interpretation (1 Cor 14:2), but where divers kinds of tongues are used there must be an interpretation (1 Cor 14:13, 28).

The Authorised Version says *'divers kinds of tongues'* (1 Cor 12:10) which means diversities of tongues or different kinds of tongues. Consequently, when this gift is in operation we can expect different languages to be coming from the same person each time. This enables us to distinguish between tongues and divers kinds of tongues in practical situations.

The Scriptures reveal that we are to expect every kind of language in the operation of this gift (1 Cor 13:1) from men to angels. They also reveal that every believer can speak in tongues but not every believer can have the gift of divers kinds of tongues (1 Cor 14:5; Acts 2:4; 1 Cor 12:10, 11, 28, 30). Paul says that a person giving a message in tongues is able to interpret himself (1 Cor 14:13) but must keep quiet if nobody or himself is able to interpret (1 Cor 14:28). Tongues are for a sign to unbelievers; no doubt to convince them of sin and the existence of God (1 Cor 14:22). Many instances have been experienced when a person has operated this gift in the presence of an unbeliever who knows the language used and has consequently surrendered his life to God. Paul gives a practical point also when this gift is in operation that like prophecy, there can only be a maximum of three messages in tongues in any one meeting which must each have an interpretation and must follow each other (1 Cor 14:27).

Finally, it must be said that prophecy is a greater gift than *'divers kinds of tongues,'* except there is an interpretation, because prophecy (or tongues combined with interpretation) edifies the whole church (1 Cor 14:4–5); however, tongues must never be forbidden in church services (1 Cor 14:39).

Interpretation of Tongues

This supernatural gift of the Holy Spirit is the supernatural interpretation into the known tongue. Notice it states interpretation and not translation (1 Cor 12:10). This is a significant point for a number of reasons. Firstly, an interpretation is far more edifying than a translation, since if it were a translation, it would not flow smoothly but rather it would be disjointed. Also, an interpretation makes the message clear so that everyone may be edified (1 Cor 14:5).

One question that arises often with regard to the operation of the gifts of tongues and interpretation is the frequent difference in length of, say, an interpretation and an utterance in tongues. There are two main reasons for this. Firstly, languages vary considerably when translating from one into another. For example, it may take four words in the English language to express one word in Greek: e.g. *'dogmatizo'* is translated 'be subject to ordinances'. Secondly, an interpretation may take far longer to express clearly than a translation like in the book of Daniel:

> *'And this is the writing that was written, MENE, MENE, TEKEL, UPHARSIN. This is the interpretation of the thing: MENE, God hath numbered thy Kingdom and finished it. TEKEL; Thou art weighed in the balances, and art found wanting. PERES; Thy Kingdom is divided, and given to the Medes and Persians.'* (Dan 5:15–28)

Notice it said 'interpretation' and had as many as eleven words to express its meaning clearly.

It must be said that this gift is absolutely supernatural and does not depend at all upon language study but is rather a miracle from the Holy Spirit of God. Also, this gift of interpretation of tongues is unique in terms of the other eight gifts of the Spirit in that it cannot be used without the gift of tongues: however, tongues and interpretation are unique in the fact that they need each other to edify the church.

An interesting point regarding the gift of interpretation is that only one person may be used for interpretation during a meeting (1 Cor 14:27, 28 – note: interpreter is singular in verse 28). This does not mean though, that there is only one interpreter for one church necessarily. Another point worthy of mention is that an interpretation to a message in tongues is equal to prophecy (1 Cor 14:5). The reasons why God has given both prophecy and tongues and interpretation and not just prophecy is firstly because it takes more faith to operate prophecy than tongues or interpretation (Rom 12:6), which means that someone who does not have enough faith for prophecy can still be used in tongues. Also, tongues are for a sign to unbelievers (1 Cor 14:22) and prophecy is used to convince unbelievers (1 Cor 14:24) which shows that even though prophecy is equivalent to tongues and interpretation, the gifts have separate uses also.

Conclusion

We have seen that God has fully equipped His church with these nine supernatural gifts of the Holy Spirit. They are needed just as much today, if not more, as during the early church. The Scriptures are very clear in this by stating that these nine manifestations will not pass away until the return of Christ (1 Cor 13:8–12) until we meet Him *'face to face'* (1 Jn 3:2). Consequently, we are to desire them and operate them for the edifying of the body of Christ and to bring glory, honour and praise to our wonderful Saviour Jesus Christ.

Chapter 7

The Five-Fold Ministry Gifts

Introduction

The word ministry comes from the Greek word *'dia-konias'* which means service. Everyone who is involved in full-time ministry for the Lord is in it to serve and not to dictate. In fact, everyone who belongs to the Body of Christ is a servant of God and has some particular part or ministry, within the church (1 Cor 12:12–27; Rom 12:4–13). Everyone within the church has the ability to be used of God to edify the rest of the body by prayers and the operation of spiritual gifts (1 Cor 14:3–5; 13–17). Personal testimony of God's dealings with people and much fruit bearing will also edify and encourage the whole body.

The greatest example of a servant is the Lord Jesus Christ (Mt 20:28; Lk 22:27; Jn 13:4–5; Phil 2:7). In Christ we see total obedience to the will of the Father (Jn 4:34; 5:30; 6:38); we see humility (Phil 2:8; Zech 9:9; Mt 11:29; 2 Cor 8:9). We see total dedication to His commission, not to mention His total separation from the things of the world and His abundant fruit bearing (2 Cor 10:1). These qualities are all essential to Christian service, and everyone would do well to *'let this mind be in you which was also in Christ Jesus'* (Phil 2:5), and to follow His ideal example (Jn 13:5; Rom 15:5; Col 3:13).

We also notice in Scripture that Christ Himself possessed the five ministries mentioned in Ephesians 4:11–12. He was and is, *'the Apostle and High Priest of our profession'* (Heb 3:1); He is the prophesied Prophet of Deuteronomy 18:15–18 (Lk 7:16; Jn 4:19; 7:40; 3:34); Christ is the greatest evangelist (Mt 4:17, 23; Lk 4:18–19); He is the *'great Shepherd of the sheep'* (Heb 13:20) which demonstrates His pastoral anointing (Jn 10:11; Is 40:11; Ps 23:1; 1 Pet 2:25; 5:4) and finally, He is the great teacher (Mt 5:2; 7:29; Mk 6:34; Lk 4:15; Jn 3:2; 8:2).

A very important point to realise about these ministry gifts is that one man who is called of God may be equipped with some or all of these ministries. Paul demonstrates all five (Rom 11:13; Acts 13:1; 15:35; 1 Cor 14:6; 1 Tim 2:7; 2 Tim 1:11), whereas other of the apostles show two or three of these ministries.

We will now examine each of the ministry gifts; apostles, prophets, evangelists, pastors and teachers.

Apostles

The meaning of the word apostle (*apostole*) is a sending or a commission i.e. an apostleship. The other New Testament word apostle (*apostolos*) means a delegate or an ambassador of the gospel, a messenger or one that is sent.

There are various kinds of apostles mentioned in the New Testament. We will discuss each one separately.

Firstly, the twelve original disciples of Jesus are called apostles (Lk 6:13–16) and are given an apostolic ministry even before they are baptized in the Holy Ghost or truly born again (Lk 9:1–2; Jn 7:37–39; 20:22). This kind of apostleship has a unique qualification in that he has to be a witness to the resurrection of Jesus (Acts 1:22). The

mission that these twelve have is to lay the initial foundations of the church (Eph 2:20) and have their eternal
reward by having their names written on the twelve
foundations of the New Jerusalem (Rev 21:14) which is
an apt title with the word 'foundations'.

Next we come to Paul who has a unique ministry. He
is definitely an apostle (Rom 1:1; 2 Cor 1:1; Gal 1:1; Eph
1:1) and He claims to be equal with the twelve apostles
(2 Cor 11:5) since he saw Jesus in a vision after the
resurrection (1 Cor 9:1; Acts 9:1–9). The reason for his
ministry being unique is two-fold; firstly, because he does
not actually see Jesus on his journey to Damascus; it is a
vision, and secondly because his gift is to be exercised to
the Gentiles and not the Jews (Acts 9:15; 22:21; Rom
11:13; Gal 2:8).

Also in Scripture we find other apostles such as
Barnabas (Acts 13:2; 14:14; 15:12) Andronicus and Junia
(Rom 16:7) who are true apostles. However, we do find
various false apostles mentioned (2 Cor 11:13; Rev 2:2)
who are self-styled and set themselves up as apostles.
This is contrary to the definition of a true apostle who is
one that is sent by God; i.e. a God-appointed office.
They would have done well to follow Paul's humble
example (1 Cor 15:9) or better still, that of Christ (Phil
2:5–8).

As we look at the various duties that apostles are
involved with we see that their duties are widespread.
They are greatly used in the supernatural realm of healing and deliverance from demon power (Lk 9:1–2; 10:17;
Mk 6:13; Acts 2:43; 5:15–16; 8:6–7, 13) which are the
signs of an apostle (2 Cor 12:12); they are also used
greatly in establishing pioneer works and missionary
work (1 Cor 3:10; Acts 14:6–23; 18:23–21:17); adminis-
tration work also is demanded of them (Acts 15:1–11)
and leadership in the spiritual gifts is also demonstrated
(Acts 8:13–17; 1 Cor 14:6).

An apostle is consequently someone who has a tremendous responsibility towards God and the church. He must be Christ-like in his actions and *'full of good fruits.'* He must expect much opposition, trials and sufferings (Acts 20:23; 1 Cor 4:11–13; 2 Cor 4:8–11; 11:23–27; Col 1:24).

Finally, it must be said that apostles are very needed today, as are the other ministries. This can only be achieved by prayerful people asking God to raise up men with the qualifications laid down in Scripture. It can also be said that there are already God-anointed Spirit-filled men of God who are performing the role of true apostles and are remaining humble enough by not labelling themselves as such.

Prophets

The definition of a prophet is an expounder of divine revelation with forthtelling and foretelling abilities in the Word; a spokesman or interpreter of deity. Forthtelling means the revelation of the will of God for the present whereas foretelling is the revealing of the future and its significance for the present situation.

In the Old Testament there are many examples of prophets such as Abraham (Gen 20:7), Moses (Deut 34:10), Nathan (2 Sam 7:2), Elijah (1 Kings 18:36), Jeremiah (Jer 1:5) and Zechariah (Zech 1:1) to mention but a few. We are also able to glean a certain amount of information regarding the role of a prophet from the Old Testament since the definition is the same as in the New Testament. The Old Testament gives us most important guidelines about the adherence to prophecy. Firstly, what is prophesied must comply with Scripture as a whole (Deut 13:1–5) and secondly, if what the prophet says comes to pass then he must be a prophet of the Lord (Deut 18:18–22). There are examples in the Word of false prophets who spoke presumptuously of themselves and not as the Spirit of the Lord anointed them. However, it must be noted that Old Testament prophecy as set down in Scripture is infallible (2 Tim 3:16; 2 Pet 1:19–21). Prophecies must always be checked against Scripture and with confirmations before acting upon them (1 Cor 14:2, 9; 1 Thess 5:21; 1 Jn 4:1).

A New Testament example of a prophet is John the Baptist (Mt 11:7–14; Mk 1:14–15; Lk 1:76–79; Jn 1:15, 29). He was filled with the Holy Spirit from his mother's womb (Lk 1:15) and spoke the oracles of God by divine revelation. His ministry was almost entirely prophetic both in foretelling and forthtelling (Mt 3:1–2, 11; Lk 3:7, 10–14). It is interesting to note the life of the prophet John the Baptist as demonstrating righteousness and holiness and most of the truly Christian attributes such as self-denial (Mt 3:4) including fasting (Mt 9:14), courage and boldness (Mt 3:7; 14:4), obedience (Mt 3:15), humility (Jn 1:19–23, 27; 3:29–31), holiness (Mk 6:20), zeal (Jn 5:35) and finally martyrdom (Mt 14:10). These qualities of a godly life must be seen in anyone who claims to have a prophetic ministry. In fact, any of the ministry gifts must be coupled with the person demonstrating Christ-likeness.

In the early church there is mention of this ministry gift (1 Cor 12:28, 29; Eph 4:11) and its application (Acts 11:27–28) which helped to relieve the church at Judaea during the famine (Acts 11:29) and also gave direction with particular appointments of service (Acts 13:1–3).

The function of the prophet is four-fold. Firstly, on a national level it is to bring a nation to repentance and back to biblical standards. Secondly, on a denominational level, to give a word to a movement for direction to the will of God. Thirdly, on a local level it is to revive an assembly. The ministry may be manifested through the revelation gifts of wisdom and knowledge or through prophecy or even through God-anointed preaching. Fourthly, on an individual level it is to give direction and wise counsel to a person about his present or future situation (1 Tim 4:14).

The Bible reveals that men and women can prophesy (Acts 21:9; 1 Cor 11:5) and in fact, anyone may prophesy (1 Cor 14:1, 5). However, the ministry of a prophet is different from the gift of prophecy but there are many similarities. Also, a person possessing the ministry of a prophet can also hold other of the ministry gifts.

Julian Ward concludes that:

'The true prophet will manifest a truly Christian life-style (Mt 7:15–20). He will have received a distinct call of God to his prophetic ministry (Rev 1:19) and will feel a deep sense of responsibility towards his hearers (1 Thess 4:13, 15; 2 Thess 2:2, 15). The validity of true prophecy will be indicated by its relevance to present action (Acts 11:29) and will be confirmed by the inner witness of the Holy Spirit (1 Jn 2:20, 27) and the corporate response of the church (1 Cor 14:29). It is by fasting and praying and waiting on the Lord that we will hear what the Spirit is saying to the churches (Acts 13:2).'

Evangelists

W.E. Vine defines an evangelist from the Greek word *'euangelistes'* as 'a messenger of good (*eu* = well; *angelos* = a messenger), it denotes a preacher of the gospel.' Although the word 'evangelist' is only used three times in the New Testament (Acts 21:8; Eph 4:11; 2 Tim 4:5) the verb is used frequently and is used by God (Gal 3:8, *'before announced glad tidings'*), by the Lord Jesus Christ

(Lk 20:1, *'announcing glad tidings'* as translated by George Ricker Berry in interlinear or in the AV *'preached the gospel'*), and by ordinary church members (Acts 8:4), as well as by the apostles on their missionary journeys.

We can, therefore, have a four-fold function of evangelists. Firstly, there are world evangelists such as Paul in the Acts of the Apostles. Secondly, national evangelists who travel just in one country or province, such as Peter in the Acts of the Apostles. Thirdly, there are assembly evangelists who 'do the work of an evangelist' just in one town, and fourthly, there are personal evangelists who should be found in every assembly; moreover, everyone should seek to be a personal evangelist.

The Scriptures reveal that there are two types of evangelists; those who have a calling from God to be a full-time evangelist like Philip (Acts 21:8) and those who do the work of an evangelist which Timothy is exhorted to be by Paul (2 Tim 4:5) even though Timothy had the call to be a pastor-teacher.

The main aim or objective of any evangelist is to lead souls to Christ using scriptural methods. Spirit-anointed preaching must always be at the centre or forefront of evangelism. Peter demonstrates this marvellously just after his baptism in the Holy Ghost (Acts 2:14–40) with the phenomenal results of three thousand converts (Acts 2:41) with more to follow (verse 47). The church is commissioned to preach the gospel to every creature (Mt 28:19–20; Mk 16:15) with miraculous signs to follow (Mk 16:17–20). It is these signs and wonders that will lead men and women to Christ as is demonstrated by Philip the evangelist (Acts 8:5–13) and by the Lord Jesus Christ (Jn 2:10–11, 23; 4:50–53; 7:31; 10:37–42). Needless to say that the qualifications of a true evangelist will almost certainly include the gifts of discerning of spirits and working of miracles to cast out devils, along with the gifts of healings to heal diseases and all manner of sickness. With these signs following he will be able to say with Paul *'through mighty signs and wonders, by the power of the Spirit of God ... I have fully preached the gospel of Christ'* (Rom 15:19; Heb 2:4).

Finally, an evangelist must be adaptable in his preaching to meet the needs of those he addresses, rather like Paul when writing to the Corinthians:

> *'And unto the Jews I became as a Jew, that I might gain the Jews; to them that are under the law, as under the law, that I might gain them that are under the law ... I am made all things to all men that I might by all means save some.'*   (1 Cor 9:20–22)

Paul gives an illustration of this when exhorting the Galatian believers (Gal 2:2). A modern day example of this would be found in missionary work. The missionaries will come across different languages, traditions and cultures, and will have to adapt their preaching accordingly. In fact, the term 'evangelist' seems to have been synonymous with the English word 'missionary', says Conybeare and Howson writing on *The Life and Epistles of St. Paul*. It can be said therefore that all missionaries do the work of an evangelist and some of them have their calling as an evangelist.

Pastors

We will discuss pastors and teachers separately, as a person cannot truly execute the role of a pastor without being a teacher, but a teacher does not necessarily have to be a pastor. This will become clear as we look at each gift.

In the New Testament there is only one reference to

the word 'pastors' (Eph 4:11) in the KJV. However, if we look at the Greek word *'poimen'* it is translated as shepherd as well as pastor (Mt 9:36; Mk 14:27; Jn 10:2, 11, 12, 14, 16; Heb 13:20; 1 Pet 2:25) with Jesus being the chief Shepherd *'archipoimen'* (1 Pet 5:4). There are other words that mean basically the same thing, such as *'episkopos'* which is translated overseer (Acts 20:28) and bishop (1 Tim 3:2; Tit 1:7; 1 Pet 2:25).

The definition of a pastor (shepherd, overseer or bishop) is; 'a shepherd, one who tends herds or flocks (not one who merely feeds them) ... Pastors guide as well as feed the flock ... this involves tender care and vigilant superintendence' says W.E. Vine.

The role of a pastor is most definitely a divine calling (2 Cor 3:6; Eph 3:7; Col 1:23; 1 Tim 1:12; 2 Tim 1:11) and anything else will not and cannot be blessed of God. This is why it is most important to make sure of one's calling before going into pastoral ministry or any area of full-time work for the Lord. The role also demands absolute humility (Mt 20:26–28), like Christ (Phil 2:5–8), to be really effective for God (Jas 4:10). In Paul's first letter to Timothy we have the exhaustive list of qualifications for taking oversight. It involves being blameless (1 Tim 3:2) i.e. unrebukeable (1 Cor 1:8; Phil 2:15; 1 Thess 5:23; 2 Pet 3:14); vigilant (watchful against danger or action of others, cautious, circumspect and sober (1 Tim3:2; 1 Pet 5:8). This portion of Scripture gives excellent guidance for the pastoral ministry (1 Tim 3:1–7). There are many other guidelines and exhortations given for pastors which should be read regularly and put into practice often (1 Tim 4:1–16; 5:1–25; 2 Tim 2:1–26; 4:1–5; Tit 1:7–16). These passages show the tremendous responsibility of pastors and their need to maintain a close spiritual walk with God to be able to *make full proof of their ministry'* (2 Tim 4:5). Giving a brief summary of these passages, a pastor should demonstrate a godly and fruit-bearing life at all times, and keep his own house disciplined and in order. He must be sound on all points of doctrine implying strongly the need for much study of the Word that he may *'rightly divide the word of truth.'* He must be able to preach anointed sermons that will edify, enrich, teach, convict and encourage his hearers as well as giving personal counsel to all those who seek his guidance. A pastor must be at the forefront in the operation of the gifts of the Spirit and be able to guide any misuse of them. He must recognise his God-given authority when dealing with problems that may arise such as gossip or heresy. Also, he must be able to give wise counsel regarding those contemplating marriage, going into the ministry or regarding a court case. In fact, the list of the duties that a pastor has to perform is endless, and those duties are extremely varied. Consequently, in all these things a pastor needs to be patient, kind, tender, gracious, loving, compassionate, sensitive, understanding, forgiving and confident. All these virtues and many more are seen in the Chief Shepherd the Lord Jesus Christ who has left us an example which we would do well to follow (Mt 9:36; Mk 1:41; 6:34; Song 1:2; 2:4; 1 Cor 11:1; Rom 13:14).

Finally, a pastor that is giving himself 'fully' to his work will see growth both spiritually and numerically. He will also realise that he will receive greater judgement and will have to give account of himself and his conduct during his ministry on earth (Jas 3:1; Heb 13:17; Acts 20:28-29).

Teachers

Vine tells us that there are three Greek words denoting a teacher in the New Testament. Firstly, *'didaskalos'* which means simply teacher or teachers; secondly, *'kalodidaskalos'* which denotes a teacher of what is good and thirdly, *'pseudodidaskalos'* which is translated a false teacher.

The Lord Jesus Christ is certainly a teacher in every sense of the word (Mt 4:23; 5:2; 7:29; Mk 6:34; Lk 4:15; Jn 7:14; 8:2) and everyone acknowledges this from his close disciples (Lk 11:1) and Nicodemus (Jn 3:2) to even His enemies, the Pharisees (Mt 22:15–16). Jesus Himself tells them that He is a teacher (Jn 13:13; note: the word 'Master' is translated from the Greek *'didaskalos'* which means teacher; also in Mt 8:19; Mk 4:38; Jn 1:38). One of the outstanding qualities that Jesus portrays in His teaching is that *'He taught them as one having authority, and not as the scribes'* (Mt 7:29). This characteristic in Christ must also be displayed by every God-called, Spirit-filled, Bible teacher it they are going to bring edification and strengthening to the Body of Christ (Acts 2:4, 14–36; Eph 3:19; 4:12–16; 1 Tim 4:11; Tit 2:15).

In the great commission given by Christ to the apostles He gives them, and every other teacher afterwards, the task of teaching (Mt 28:19–20) for He knows that teaching is most important for every Christian. Jesus also teaches that the third person of the Trinity would be a teacher (Jn 14:26; 16:13); John bears witness to this fact in his first epistle (1 Jn 2:20, 27).

In the Acts of the Apostles we find that teaching is at the forefront, beginning with the first converts at Jerusalem (Acts 2:42); then we find five teachers in the church at Antioch who are also prophets (Acts 13:1; 15:35). We then see Paul pioneering the Corinthian church and establishing it by staying and teaching the Word of God eighteen months (Acts 18:1–11, esp. verse 11). In the same chapter we read of a Jew named Apollos who was *'mighty in the Scriptures'* and *'fervent in the spirit'* and *'spake and taught diligently the things of the Lord'* who spoke boldly in the synagogue even though he only knew about John's baptism (Acts 18:24–28). This man certainly demonstrates the kind of teaching that the church needs in any age. Any Bible teacher would do well to follow his example. Paul concludes the book of Acts by dwelling in a house for two years and preaching and teaching with **all confidence** the things concerning Christ and the Kingdom (Acts 28:30, 31).

The Scriptures reveal that teachers are to pass on their knowledge and teach others to teach (2 Tim 2:2), which is the main reason for Bible colleges. Ministers of any calling are to be able to teach (1 Tim 3:2) and must teach sound doctrine (1 Tim 4:6, 13, 16; 5:17) which only comes through living a godly life (1 Tim 6:11) and studying to divide the Word correctly (2 Tim 2:15).

The greatest teacher in the New Testament is Paul the apostle, except for Jesus, who taught so much in the New Testament. In fact, Paul wrote at least thirteen out of the twenty seven books contained therein, all of which are teaching epistles. He teaches concerning virtually every aspect of doctrine (the book of Romans, first and second epistles of Timothy and Titus) including eschatological discourses (1 Thess 4:13–17; 1 Cor 15:51–53), pre-destination (Rom 8:29–30; Eph 1:5, 11), the gifts of the Spirit (1 Cor 12, 13, 14) and marriage (1 Cor 7) as well as dealing with domestic affairs and problems that arise in the church (1 Tim 1:19, 20; 5:18–19; 2 Tim 2:16–17). In other words Paul teaches about everything, and so should every Bible teacher be able to so that he may be able to *'answer every man'* (Col 4:6).

Finally, the ideal Bible teacher needs to be able to teach not only babes to grow to full maturity (1 Cor 3:1–3; 1 Pet 2:2) but also deliver meat to those who are mature (1 Cor 2:13, 15; Heb 5:12–14), so that everyone may grow up into Him that is the head even Christ, and all may be good soldiers fighting the good fight of faith (Eph 4:15; 1 Tim 6:12).

Conclusion

Consequently, it is necessary for every minister to make his *'calling and election sure'* (2 Pet 1:10) by seeking the face of the Lord and understanding what the will of the Lord is for his own particular life (Eph 5:17). When a person has been called into full-time work it may not be obvious at first what his calling is; therefore pastoring a church for a while is perhaps the best training ground to begin with to enable a person to see where their various gifts lie.

The Church as a whole can also play an important role with regard to the five-fold ministry gifts by praying that God would raise men up, and that the ones concerned would recognise their calling and would be equipped with wisdom to fulfil their specific calling to the glory of God.

Chapter 8

Deliverance

As we look through the four Gospels, Matthew, Mark, Luke and John, we see that Jesus encounters demonic spirits almost everywhere He goes. These evil spirits recognise His authority immediately and often begin tearing their victims or causing them to froth at the mouth. Jesus is very simple and direct in the way He deals with all such encounters. He **casts them out by His word**. At the end of Mark's Gospel, in the Great Commission to the Church, Jesus says this very clearly:

> '*And these signs shall follow them that believe: in my name shall they cast out devils: they shall speak with new tongues.*' (Mk 16:17)

When you have been involved in deliverance ministry for any length of time you soon realise why tongues and deliverance are mentioned together. This phenomenon was usual in the life and ministry of Jesus and He obviously expects deliverance to be just as usual and commonplace today.

What are Demons?

The Bible tells us that one third of the angels fell from heaven led by their captain Lucifer (Satan) (Ezek 28:11–19; Is 14:4–23). These demons are now on earth seeking to gain control of people so that they can manifest themselves to the full. They will obviously try to gain entry into the highest levels of intelligence and thus cause as much devastation as possible. We see the very nature of Satan through people today in every kind of manner and at all levels of society. Ephesians 6:12 says:

> *'For we wrestle not against flesh and blood, but against principalities, against powers, against the rulers of the darkness of this world, against spiritual wickedness in high places.'*

What is Their Work?

Jesus says in John 10:10:

> *'The thief cometh not, but for to steal, and to kill, and to destroy: I am come that they might have life, and that they might have it more abundantly.'*

This verse is probably the best description of the work of evil spirits which is obviously directly opposed to God's Word and His standards. For instance, God's Word declares that God hates divorce (Mal 2:16). The reason why divorce is so rampant in our world today, is because Satan and his demons have been busy destroying the fibre of our society and getting people to hate each other. Divorce is largely the work of evil spirits attacking people, which obviously has a knock-on effect throughout society, thus causing financial ruin, divided families, bitter and resentful children and great

oppression. We only have to take one look at today's society to see exactly what the works of evil spirits are.

Are There Different Kinds of Spirits?

Not only are there different kinds of evil spirits (e.g. lust, envy, pride, unbelief, rejection, witchcraft etc.) but also there are different levels of demons. Then there are demons which directly cause sickness or infirmity (e.g. dumb, deaf and blind spirits).

How Do Demons Gain Entry to the Victims?

Firstly, if a person, Christian or otherwise, becomes engrossed in sin and continues for any length of time in known sin, then that person after a while will become oppressed. The longer the person continues to yield to that sin, the more of a foothold it gives to stronger spirits. We only need to examine 2 Peter 2:20–22 to see the final result of a backslider who continues in sin. That is why we need to be holy and clean and repent of all known sin to keep ourselves from oppression.

The occult (e.g. ouija board, dungeons and dragons, freemasonry, spiritism or any kind of spiritual activity which is unscriptural) will certainly attract evil spirits and needs to be repented of and renounced in the Name of Jesus Christ. Deuteronomy 18:9–14 gives a fairly comprehensive list of occult activity.

The Bible says that Satan is the most subtle of all the created beings, and therefore his deceptive techniques are very sinister. I remember ministering to a lady once in Manchester who was obviously bound in some way by evil spirits. I asked her if she had ever had any involvement with any kind of occult, which she denied. I then went through the deliverance questionnaire which we use in all such cases and she ticked yes to almost every occult practice going! She thought that it was normal and perfectly acceptable. She would practise palmistry and read Tarot cards at Church of England jumble sales! Since she had become a born-again Christian and had been baptised in the Holy Spirit, strange things had begun to happen in her house. Demonic manifestations took place in the home and she assumed that it was the house that needed deliverance. Sometimes we need to cleanse a house by taking authority in the Name of Jesus Christ and using the Blood of Jesus. However, it is usually the people who need deliverance. This is another of the devil's tactics to distract our attention from the real issue.

Another instance that shows how Satan blinds people from the truth happened recently when two Mormons came to see me. They were from Salt Lake City in Utah which is the home of Mormonism, also known as the 'Church of Jesus Christ of Latter Day Saints'. They wanted to ask me a few questions about the way that we do things in our church and having been to two of our meetings wished to talk with me about our beliefs. Having had dealings with Mormons on several previous occasions I asked them a simple question about free-masonry. They had never even heard of it. Mormonism has freemasonry at its roots and they had never heard of it. The Founder of Mormonism became a freemason towards the end of his life and intertwined the cult with all kinds of masonic rituals and emblems. No wonder Satan is called a deceiver in the Bible.

Another of Satan's deceptions is to say that once a person becomes a Christian they do not need any deliverance. Nothing could be further from the truth. Christians often need deliverance from oppressive spirits, hereditary bondages, curses, past involvements, rejection, rape, fear, abuse (verbal and sexual). The list is endless. You never know how many worms there are until you open the can! I have been surprised on many an occasion how much intensive deliverance a person has needed before they are free.

Is it Always Right to Cast Out a Devil Immediately?

In Acts 16:16–18 we have the story of the girl who has a spirit of divination (or python). She brings her employers a lot of money by fortune telling. This girl apparently attaches herself to Paul and his companions for 'many days' before Paul casts out the evil spirit. There have been times in our ministry when a person has obviously needed deliverance but was not ready for deliverance at that stage; one of the usual reasons for this is often that the person is holding on to unforgiveness or unbelief in some way. Repentance from sin or a wrong attitude will be necessary. Disobedience can also be a reason why a spirit refuses to leave. There are times when a demon will only leave when you have accurately discerned its name. The gift of discerning of spirits is crucial to know if a spirit is ready to leave. There are never two cases alike! Every case is different, even when you cast out the same sort of spirit from two different people. One of the biggest challenges with a new case is often to find a starting point. With some people you have to gently help them to come to the place where they accept such ministry. Getting someone started is often the hardest part of setting someone free.

Finally, there are some spirits which do not look as if they are ready to come out because there is no response to one person's authority. There are times when we need someone else to come in who has more experience and also a greater revelation of the authority they have in this area.

'This kind cometh not out but by prayer and fasting.'
(Mt 17:21)

Jesus rebukes His disciples for their unbelief in deliverance, which is also another important point. We must approach deliverance ministry with absolute **faith** in God's Word and in the Name of Jesus Christ. Fasting and praying much in tongues are also vital ingredients for a successful ministry of setting the captives free. Notice that Jesus began His ministry with 40 days of prayer and fasting. He did not have to keep going away and fasting every time He met demons. He was already 'fasted up' and 'prayed up', ready to deal with anything.

In the 13 years that I have been involved in this kind of ministry I have fasted regularly – sometimes up to three days at a time – and have prayed for long periods in the Holy Spirit. I usually fast every week, often twice, just to keep me in tune at all times and ready for when the Holy Spirit calls upon me.

I must emphasise at this stage that receiving deliverance ministry on its own, is not sufficient for a victorious Christian life. Before a person is delivered, during deliverance, afterwards, and for the rest of their lives they need constant Bible teaching. We need to be full of the Word – in our minds firstly and then in meditation on the Word until it becomes a reality in our hearts. This is what is known as '**revelation knowledge of the Word**'. Having a head knowledge of God's Word is not enough. Faith in God's Word is a revelation in our heart. That is why many people are leading defeated Christian lives even though they quote Scripture all day long. God's Word has to take root inside us and become the **living Word** to us. Also, once you have a revelation of God's Word about something you can no longer remain neutral. You have to **act upon that revelation**!

Does There Have to be an Obvious Manifestation to Show That a Demon Has Left?

When we are dealing with spirits at the lowest level, or some spirits of oppression, there are no obvious manifestations. Sometimes the person being ministered to knows that it has gone without there always being a manifestation. In most of the cases that I have dealt with, however, there have usually been one or more of the following physical manifestations: coughing (very common), screaming, sighing, sneezing, crying, burping, facial contortions, eyes flickering, groaning, yawning. Also certain demons will try to talk through the person and hold a conversation with you. This is a stalling tactic. Tell them to shut up and to come out in **Jesus' Name**.

Do We Ever Go Demon Hunting?

You never need to go looking for demons. They usually come looking for you!

What is the Outcome of Deliverance Ministry?

Have you ever wondered why a particular person is not growing spiritually as you would have expected? Why do some people struggle for years in the area of the fruit of the Spirit and the gifts of the Spirit? Why do some people, who should be preaching, teaching or acting in some position of leadership within the church, always want to take a back seat and refuse leadership opportunities? The answer may be that the person is sinning and does not want to stop. It could be that they simply have not yielded their lives fully to the Lord, or that **they need**

to be set free from the powers of darkness! It is wonderful to see a person who has never grown in the fruits, gifts or revelation knowledge of the Word beginning to develop in these areas once the 'troublemakers' have been cast out. Note: Demons will only go when they are **told to go** and when the person is willing to let them go. As a person is in the process of being delivered the Word of God begins to take on a new meaning. The 'penny' begins to drop. Instead of the Word being simply 'head knowledge' it becomes reality in the heart. I know someone who was undergoing deliverance ministry who actually received a call from the Lord during this time. While this person was preaching, the call of God literally 'fell' upon him and this person was changed into a new person. Glory to God!

You never know what changes God has in store for you once you have been set free to serve Christ.

Who is Qualified to Exercise Deliverance to Others?

Only those who are truly born again and are baptised in the Holy Spirit and speak in other tongues should minister deliverance. Also, they should be leading a holy life, having repented of all known sin. They need to be full of God's Word to produce strong faith since 'faith' comes by hearing and hearing by the Word of God (Rom 10:17). Anyone ministering deliverance should also fast regularly to stay in tune with the Holy Spirit. Another key to successful deliverance ministry is to be in absolute obedience both to the written Word and to the Holy Spirit's leading. Also, those ministering deliverance need to be well established in a local church and acting under the authority of the leadership of that church. The setting up of a team within the local church to minister deliverance is probably the best way of handling this vital and needy area of Christian work. This ministry is definitely not the work for just one person within a church, as it is very demanding and physically tiring. Finally, it is essential that all those seeking to minister deliverance should know **who they are in Christ Jesus**. The devil responds to authority. The devil knows if you know that you are the *'righteousness of God in Christ'* (2 Cor 5:21). The following is a brief list of who we are according to the New Testament. We are:

- The righteousness of God in Christ (2 Cor 5:21)
- Saved by the blood of Jesus (1 Pet 1:18, 19)
- Delivered from Satan's dark kingdom (Col 1:13)
- Forgiven and set free from condemnation (Eph 1:7; Rom 8:1)
- Cleansed by the blood of Jesus (1 Jn 1:7)
- Seated in heavenly places with Christ Jesus (Eph 2:6)
- Accepted in the beloved (Eph 1:6)
- Reconciled to God through Christ (2 Cor 5:18)
- Redeemed from the curse of the law (Gal 3:13)
- Kings and Priests unto our God (Rev 1:5, 6)
- Partakers of God's very nature (2 Pet 1:3, 4)
- A son of God (Jn 1:12)
- Ambassadors for Christ (2 Cor 5:20)
- God's workmanship (Eph 2:10)
- Inseparable from God's love (Rom 8:38, 39)

1 Jn 4:17 says it all when God says:

*'As He is, so are **we in this world**.'*

This verse says that we should be just like Jesus Himself when He walked this earth. The demons should respond to us the same way that they responded to Jesus. Hallelujah! On one occasion an evil spirit spoke through a man to the seven sons of Sceva and said:

*'Jesus I know and Paul I know: but **who are ye?'***
(Acts 19:15)

Let us make sure that we know who we are in Christ because we would not want to end up like these men in this story! (See Acts 19:13–17.)

To conclude this chapter I want to give a brief list of evil spirits that are mentioned in the Bible:

1. Divination or Python (fortune telling etc.) (Acts 16:16).
2. Jezebel (controlling, domineering spirit) (Rev 2:20).
3. Legion (Mk 5:9; Lk 8:30).
4. Doctrines of devils (false cults and sects) (1 Tim 4:1).
5. Jealous spirit (used twice) (Num 5:14, 30).
6. A foul spirit (used twice) (Mk 9:25; Rev 18:2).
7. Binding spirit (Mt 18:18).
8. Seducing spirits (1 Tim 4:1).
9. A lying spirit (used 4 times) (1 Kings 22:22, 23; 2 Chron 18:21, 22).
10. A dragon (Rev 12:7–9).
11. A lion (1 Pet 5:8).
12. An angel of light (2 Cor 11:14).
13. Familiar spirits (Lev 20:27; Is 8:19; 2 Kings 23:24).
14. Blind spirit (Mt 12:22).
15. Unclean spirit (used 22 times) (Mt 12:43; Mk 1:23; Lk 9:42).
16. Dumb and deaf spirit (Mk 9:25).
17. Spirit of infirmity (Lk 13:11).

This is by no means a complete list as anyone involved in this ministry will tell you. There are, literally, hundreds of different types of evil spirits. No wonder Jesus says as part of the **great commission** *'In my name you shall cast out devils!'* (Mk 16:17).

Chapter 9

Faith

As we take a tour through the Gospels we shall see just how much emphasis Jesus puts on faith.

> 'Wherefore, if God so clothes the grass of the field, which today is, and tomorrow is cast into the oven, shall he not much more clothe you, **O ye of little faith**?' (Mt 6:30)

> 'When Jesus heard it, He marvelled, and said to them that followed, verily I say unto you, I have not found **so great faith**, no not in Israel.' (Mt 8:10; Lk 7:9)

> 'And, behold, they brought to Him a man sick of the palsy; lying on a bed: and Jesus **seeing their faith** said unto the sick of the palsy: Son, be of good cheer: thy sins be forgiven thee.' (Mt 9:2)

> 'But Jesus turned Him about, and when He saw her, He said, Daughter, be of good comfort; **thy faith hath made thee whole**, And the woman was made whole from that hour.' (Mt 9:22)

> 'Then touched He their eyes, saying, According to **your faith be it unto you**.' (Mt 9:29)

*'And immediately Jesus stretched forth His hand, and caught him, and said unto him, **O thou of little faith**, wherefore didst thou doubt?'* (Mt 14:31)

*'Then Jesus answered and said unto her, O woman, **great is thy faith**: be it unto thee even as thou wilt. And her daughter was made whole from that very hour.'* (Mt 15:28)

*'Which when Jesus perceived, He said unto them, **O ye of little faith**, why **reason** ye among yourselves, because ye have brought no bread?'* (Mt 16:8)

*'And Jesus said unto them, because of **your unbelief**; for verily I say unto you, If ye have **faith as a grain of mustard seed, ye shall say unto this mountain**, remove hence to yonder place; and it shall remove; **and nothing shall be impossible unto you**.'*

(Mt 17:20, see also Mt 21:21)

*'And He said unto them, Why are ye so fearful? How is it that **ye have no faith**?'* (Mk 4:40)

*'And He said unto her Daughter, **thy faith hath made thee whole**; go in peace, and be whole of thy plague.'*

(Mk 5:34, see also Mk 19:52)

*'And Jesus answering saith unto them, **have faith in God**.'* (Margin) *'have the faith of God.'*

(Mk 11:22, see verses 23, 24)

*'And He said unto them, **"Where is your faith?"** And they being afraid wondered, saying one to another, what manner of man is this! for He commandeth even the winds and water, and they obey him.'* (Lk 8:25)

*'But I have prayed for thee, that **thy faith fail not**: and when thou art converted, strengthen thy brethren.'*

(Lk 22:32)

110

Jesus knew the importance of faith for the power of God to be effective in people's lives. Doubt, fear and unbelief were commonplace wherever Jesus went and sadly, the same is true today. God is looking for a people of faith who will once again *'be strong and do exploits'* (Dan 11:32).

Three Types of Faith

1. Faith to believe unto salvation (Eph 2:8).
2. The fruit of the Spirit faith (Gal 5:22). (See chapter on fruit.)
3. The gift of the Spirit faith (1 Cor 12:9). (See chapter on the gifts of the Spirit.)

Faith to Believe Unto Salvation

When the gospel is preached to an unsaved person God gives that person faith to become a Christian. Unfortunately, many Christians never develop beyond this initial experience of faith and consequently lead a very low-level spiritual life. This, however, is not what God wants at all. God wants us all moving into strong depths of both the fruit of faith and the miraculous realm of the supernatural gift of faith.

Two Kinds of Faith

1. Sense-knowledge faith (based on the five physical senses).
2. Real Bible faith.

Sense-knowledge faith is not really faith at all. It is what the world calls faith. John Wesley said that sense-knowledge faith is really called **'mental assent'**. It has its roots in the five physical senses namely, sight, hearing, touch, smell and taste. We have often heard the statement 'I will only believe when I have seen it for myself.' Unfortunately, even though this is the world's philosophy, many born-again Christians have been deceived by the devil through mental assent and unbelief. You often hear Christians say: 'I will believe that I am healed when I feel healed; then I will praise God.'

Even though the word 'believe' is in this statement it is not a statement of faith at all as we will now see.

The Queen of Sheba

In 1 Kings 10:1–13, we have a graphic illustration of sense-knowledge faith in the life of the Queen of Sheba. Solomon is becoming famous and his popularity has gained the attention of this pagan Queen. She has been told of the wisdom, wealth and fame of Solomon but she admits that she will not believe until she has seen it for herself:

> *'And she said to the King, It was a true report that I heard in mine own land of thy acts and of thy wisdom. Howbeit **I believed not the words, until I came, and mine eyes had seen it**: and, behold, the half was not told me: thy wisdom and prosperity exceedeth the fame which I heard.'* (verses 6, 7)

This is a classic example of unbelief; when you are told something is true but flatly refuse to believe until you have seen it for yourself. In the New Testament we have a similar character who demonstrates how unbelief operates. Note, this is one of Jesus' personal staff members – **Thomas**!

> *'But Thomas, one of the twelve, called Didymus, was not with them when Jesus came. The other disciple*

112

*therefore said unto him, We have seen the Lord. But he said unto them, Except I shall **see in His hands** the print of the nails, and **put my finger** into the print of the nails, and **thrust my hand** into His side, **I will not believe.'** (Jn 20:24, 25)*

One thing is certain: Thomas was extremely well established in unbelief. He was consistent in what he didn't believe! Even though this attitude must have saddened Jesus He still took the time and patience to teach Thomas about faith and believing. Thank God He is patient with us all! Eight days later Jesus walked through the walls to be with His team and announces: *'Peace be unto you.'* Straight away He focuses in on Thomas and says:

*'Reach hither thy finger, and behold my hands: and reach hither thy hand, and thrust it into my side: and be not **faithless**, but **believing.'** (Jn 20:27)*

Thomas must have felt about as small as a mouse in front of his colleagues.

'And Thomas answered and said unto him, My Lord and my God.' (verse 28)

*'Jesus saith unto him, Thomas, **because thou hast seen me, thou has believed: Blessed are they that have not seen, and yet have believed.'*** (verse 29)

Which category do you fit into? Are you always having to see or feel before you will believe or is God's Word sufficient evidence to generate faith in your heart? We need to grow out of sense-knowledge faith as quickly as possible and move into real faith that moves mountains.

Real Bible Faith

The Bible actually gives us a definition of what real faith is. Hebrews 11:1 says:

> *'Now faith is the substance* (Margin: ground or confidence) *of things hoped for, the evidence of things not seen* (or *not yet revealed to the senses'*, Amplified).

Sense-knowledge faith says 'I will believe it only when I see it!' Genuine Bible faith says 'I believe it therefore I shall see it!'

When Jesus is about to raise Lazarus from the dead He makes this statement of faith unto Martha:

> *'... Said I not unto thee, that, if thou wouldest **believe**, thou shouldest **see** the **glory of God**?'*
>
> (Jn 11:40)

The believing always comes first. Many unsaved people have said that they will only believe in God when they have seen Him. Such people are deceived because the only way into the Kingdom of God is by faith through grace (Eph 2:8). God's grace gives and our faith receives. Paul makes a tremendous declaration of faith in the second letter to the Corinthians:

> *'While we look not at the things which are **seen**, but at the things which are not seen: for the things which are seen are temporal* (i.e. subject to change): *but the things which are not seen are eternal.'*
>
> (2 Cor 4:18)

Once we become truly born-again Christians we have to learn to *'Walk by faith, not by sight'* (2 Cor 5:7) because the only true way to please our Heavenly Father is by faith.

> '*Now the just shall* **live by faith**: *but if any man draw back, my soul shall have no pleasure in him.*'
>
> (Heb 10:38)

> '*But* **without faith it is impossible to please Him**: *for he that cometh to God must believe that* **He is**, *and that He is a rewarder of them that diligently seek Him.*'
>
> (Heb 11:6)

Therefore, living a life of faith is not really an option but a commandment of God for our benefit so that we can live the life on earth that God intends for us to live – a life of victory and success, excitement, challenge, blessing and glory.

What we need to do is to fill our minds and hearts with God's Word and whenever we find something hard to believe we should stop and repent of **unbelief** in our heart and renounce it and receive faith for that particular part of our life. Simply having a head knowledge of something in God's Word is not sufficient to make it work in our lives.

> '*For unto us was the gospel preached, as well as unto them: but* **the word preached did not profit them, not being mixed with faith** *in them that heard it.*'
>
> (Heb 4:2)

We have to mix faith with what we hear from God's Word to make it profitable to us. This is why some people come to Christ and some people don't. Also, this is sometimes a reason why some people get healed and some people don't. People who are sick need to be under constant teaching from God's Word regarding healing until faith rises in their heart to the point where they can confess with their mouth 'I believe that I was healed by the stripes of Jesus' (1 Pet 2:24).

We use the phrase 'the penny has dropped' to mean that a person has finally understood something. The same is true of faith. **Faith is a revelation**. Satan is the one who will try to prevent believers (so-called believers) from getting this revelation of faith. The devil is happy with Christians who do not have this real heart revelation of faith. As soon as a Christian comes under real faith teaching, however, he tries everything to stop him from hearing it. Satan must tremble at the thought of every Christian having a full revelation of faith in their hearts. Smith Wigglesworth once said that God would by-pass a thousand Christians praying in unbelief to answer one Christian praying in faith! Are you praying in faith? Do you have a real revelation of faith to know that when you pray God will answer?

John wrote in his first letter:

> *'For whatsoever is born of God **overcometh the world**: and **this is the victory** that overcometh the world, **even our faith**.'* (1 Jn 5:4)

Jesus wants us to be world-overcomers and not overcome by the world! He has destined us to *'reign in life through one **Christ Jesus**'* (Rom 5:17). Jesus wants us living in such victory that the devil trembles every time we pray! Instead, many Christians live their lives as if circumstances are their biggest problem. The Word of God says you can change your circumstances by praying in faith! All our circumstances are subject to change by the power of God. Sadly, many Christians are defeated by their circumstances because they do not act on the Word of God relevant to their situation. God has an answer for every situation we face in life and can give you victory no matter what you are facing.

> *'Now thanks be unto God, which **always causeth us to triumph in Christ**, and maketh manifest the savour of **His knowledge by us** in every place.'*   (2 Cor 2:14)

Where Does Faith Come From?

Paul says in Romans:

> *'So then **faith cometh** by **hearing**, and **hearing** by the Word of God.'*   (Rom 10:17)

The word 'hearing' comes from a primitive verb which can be translated 'understand'. Jesus says in Mark 4:12:

> *'That seeing they may see, **and not perceive**: and hearing they may hear, **and not understand**.'*

Modern technology enables us to listen to God's Word on the cassette tape which is extremely useful. I remember when I heard the message of faith for the very first time many years ago. I understood a little bit to start with and so I bought the four cassette tapes and listened to the message of faith over and over again. Each time I listened my understanding of faith grew. I realised that I could throw mountains into the sea! (Mk 11:23). I also realised that I could no longer live a defeated Christian life and to live anything other than a victorious life was now history.

The Word of God should become top priority to us on a daily basis. Satan always fights the Word and will often distract you from having your devotional time in the Word and prayer. You have to be determined to have that time in His Word and not to listen to the lies of the

enemy. The devil knows that you are at you most danger-
ous to the kingdom of darkness when you are **full of
God's Word**. We need to read God's Word, meditate it
regularly, dwell on it, soak it up like a sponge, inwardly
digest it and then **act on it**!

James tells us:

> *'But be ye **doers of the word**, and not hearers only,
> deceiving your own selves.'*   (Jas 1:22)

Once you have heard the Word, the only way to learn
and to become established in faith is to do it! Once you
begin to act on God's Word in any area of life you will
have to stand on God's Word until what you are believing for comes to pass. Often the circumstances look
worse before they turn around for good. This is just the
devil trying to make the situation look bad and to get
you to say 'It is not working.' The devil loves to hear
those words. Faith never says that. Even in the face of
disaster faith still says 'It is working because God is with
me.'

How is Faith Released?

It is one thing to have faith built up in your heart. All the
time it is inside you it won't do anything for you until
you release it out of your **mouth**. Faith is therefore
released through our mouth. It is commonly referred to
as our confession of faith. Faith is spoken.

> *'We having the same spirit of faith, according as it is
> written, I believed, and therefore have I spoken: **We
> also believe, and therefore speak**.'*   (2 Cor 4:13)

This is how God released (and releases) His faith and
that is how we release our faith. We will always speak

what we believe either good or bad, negative or positive. We have to learn to speak good things only and not bad things. We must also learn to speak positive things only and not negative. The Word of God says:

> '*O generation of vipers, how can ye, being evil, **speak good things? For out of the abundance of the heart the mouth speaketh**.*' (Mt 12:34)

Jesus goes on to say:

> '*A good man out of the good treasure of the heart bringeth forth good things: and an evil man out of the evil treasure bringeth forth evil things. But I say unto you, That every idle word that men shall speak, they shall give account thereof in the day of judgment. For **by thy words thou shalt be justified**, and **by thy words thou shalt be condemned**.*' (Mt 12:35–37)

In the light of this sobering teaching by Jesus Himself it must be obvious that we must guard what goes into our heart so that only good things come out. The mind is a very powerful human faculty. It remembers many things. What we need to do is to make sure that only good things are going into our ears, eyes, mind and then heart in order for us to speak only good things. If the company that you are surrounded with is always saying evil and negative things then you need to change the company that you keep. Paul the apostle says:

> '*Be not deceived: evil communications corrupt good manners.*' (1 Cor 15:33)

We see the importance of believing in our heart and confessing with our mouth right at the start of our Christian experience.

> *'But what saith it? The word is nigh thee, even in **thy mouth**, and **in thy heart**: that is, the word of faith, which we preach: That if thou shalt **confess** with **thy mouth** the **Lord Jesus**, and shalt **believe in thine heart** that God hath raised Him from the dead, thou shalt be saved. For with the **heart man believeth unto** righteousness: and **with the mouth confession** is made unto salvation.'* (Rom 10:8–10)

In the very beginning we can see that God used faith to create the heavens and the earth (Heb 11:3). In the first chapter of Genesis we read:

> *'And God **said**, Let the earth bring forth grass, the herb yielding seed, and the fruit tree yielding fruit after his kind, whose seed is in itself, upon the earth: **and it was so.**'* (Gen 1:11)

As far as God was concerned it was done as soon as He had **spoken**. As yet, however, nothing could be seen. God actually said that it was even before it was revealed to the senses. Verse 12 then says:

> *'And the earth brought forth grass, and herb yielding seed after his kind, and the tree yielding fruit, whose seed was in itself, after his kind: and God **saw** that it was good.'*

See verses 14–16 also.

In the story of Abraham we see exactly the same principle of faith in operation.

> *'(As it is written, **I have made thee** a father of many nations) before him whom he believed, even God, who quickeneth the dead, and **calleth those things which be***

*not as though they were. Who against hope believed in hope, that he might become the father of many nations, according to that which was **spoken, so shall thy seed be**. And being not weak in faith, he considered not his own body now dead, when he was about an hundred years old, neither yet the deadness of Sarah's womb: **He staggered not** at the promise of God through unbelief: but was **strong in faith**, giving glory to God: And being **fully persuaded** that, what He had promised, He was able also to perform.'*

(Rom 4:17–21)

Abraham could have considered many things other than what God had said. Sarah had had no children because she was barren and had been all her life. Faith believes God's Word and speaks it out of the mouth. Note that it took Abraham 29 years to come to that place of absolute faith. Abraham made many mistakes before he became established in strong faith. Like Abraham, once our faith has been released out of our mouth we then have to guard our confession until the full manifestation is seen in the physical. This 'standing time' (Eph 6:13) develops one of the most important characteristics of God in our lives – consistency. God is the most consistent being as demonstrated in the life and ministry of Jesus Christ. Jesus was consistent in His earthly life in all that He did. He was consistently victorious. He maintained a consistent walk with His Father. He was consistently positive. He was consistently obedient which showed His absolute love and devotion to the Father's will. Jesus walked totally by faith and left us an example to walk as He walked (1 Jn 2:6).

'If any of you lack wisdom, let him ask of God, that giveth to all men liberally, and upbraideth not: and it

121

*shall be given him. But **let him ask in faith, nothing wavering**. For he that wavereth is like a wave of the sea driven with the wind and tossed. For let not that man think that he shall receive anything of the Lord. **A double minded man is unstable in all** his ways.'*

(Jas 1:5–8)

Let us all learn to walk by faith every day and become steadfast and unmoved by anything contrary to God's Word (1 Cor 15:58).

Faith for Every Area of Life

The Word of God tells us that:

*'The just shall **live** by faith.'*   (Rom 1:17)

This verse strongly suggests that the whole of our life and everything that we do should be by faith. Unfortunately, many precious Christians are using their faith simply for their salvation. This is not what God intended. God wants us to use our faith to give us success in every aspect of life. A garden would look very peculiar if only part of it was well-pruned and the lawn was only partly-cut. The Lord has provided victory in every area of our life. (Psalm 1 for instance.) There are some Christians who have well-exercised faith for healing but struggle in the area of finances. Others trust God for both and speak ugly about their partner. If ever there was an area of our life where we need to use our faith constantly it is in marriage. Every Christian couple should seek to have a marriage which gets better every day. You can only do that by faith.

Faith for Personal Evangelism

> *'For I am not ashamed of the gospel of Christ; for it is the power of God unto salvation to everyone that believeth: to the Jew first, and also to the Greek.'*
>
> (Rom 1:16)

I am amazed at the number of Spirit-filled Christians who find it hard to share their faith with others. This is unbelief in personal evangelism and usually stems from a poor self-image. I have never had that problem. I began to tell others about Jesus Christ the day I found Him myself. I still look forward to Divine appointments of personal evangelism to this day. Even though most of my time is spent with believers I still seize every opportunity to tell people about Jesus Christ. **It is a command** and **not an option**.

> *'Go ye into all the world, and preach the gospel to every creature.'*
>
> (Mk 16:15)

> *'But ye shall receive power, after that the Holy Spirit is come upon you: and ye shall **be witnesses** unto me both in Jerusalem, and in all Judaea, and in Samaria, and unto the uttermost part of the earth.'*
>
> (Acts 1:8)

> *'For though I preach the gospel, I have nothing to glory of: for necessity is laid upon me: yea **woe is unto me, if I preach not the gospel!'***
>
> (1 Cor 9:16)

There are some people who try to wriggle out of their responsibility of personal evangelism by making such statements as 'that's not my calling in the Body of Christ.' We are not all set in the ministry gifting of the Evangelist but we are all called to personal evangelism.

123

There are some people who will only listen to you! Are you going to let those people down? This is a vital area that needs to be addressed in many Christian's lives.

Personal evangelism gets your eyes off you and your little world and onto other people who are going to a Christless eternity. We are the ones who can do something about it! I get more enjoyment from sharing Jesus with one lost soul than just about anything. It is the most exciting ministry available and we can all do it! Don't let a week go by without sharing the good news of Jesus with somebody. People will listen to you. Don't go around saying that nobody wants to listen to you. Repent of that negative attitude and start to see yourself as God sees you. A good confession of faith for evangelism that you can say every day is this:

'I make myself available to you Father today to be a witness. I can witness to anybody that you put into my path. I believe that I have the wisdom to answer questions by the Holy Spirit who lives in me. I look forward to telling someone today. Thank you Father for sending them to me, in Jesus' name.'

One of the most awesome passages in the Bible for a Christian to read must be Ezekiel 33. Here is a sample for you to ponder on the seriousness of personal evangelism:

'So thou, O son of man, I have set thee a watchman unto the house of Israel; therefore thou shalt hear the word at my mouth, and **warn them from me**. When I say unto the wicked, O wicked man, thou shalt surely die; if **thou dost not speak to warn the wicked** from his way, that wicked man shall die in his iniquity: **but his blood will I require at thine hand.'** (verses 7–8)

124

Personal evangelism keeps our eyes on the important issues of life. It keeps us prayerful and watchful over our own lives. Satan is the one trying to stop us from fulfilling this basic responsibility we have of telling others of Jesus. Use your authority over him and give him a surprise by telling people about Jesus! More people become Christians through personal evangelism than by any other method of outreach. Over 80% of those born-again were reached through personal evangelism, and they can then be discipled and become committed to the church. Sheep bring sheep. Don't leave this to others. **Do it yourself!**

Faith to Hear the Voice of the Lord

As you develop in your personal walk of faith and start acting on God's written Word you will begin to hear God's voice speaking to you personally. We need to have faith for this to start happening today. Job says:

> *'For God speaketh once, yea twice, yet man perceiveth it not.'* (Job 33:14, see to verse 17)

God is obviously far more willing to speak to us than we are ready to hear! We ought to prepare our hearts and have faith to believe that God will speak to us. Expect to hear His voice in the Name of Jesus!

Faith for Revival

> *'And it shall come to pass afterward, that I will pour out my spirit upon all flesh . . . '* (Joel 2:28–32)

It is one thing to use our faith for our needs to be met (Phil 4:19) and for our healing (1 Pet 2:24) and for personal evangelism, success at work, a happy marriage

125

and blessed children but we must not be selfish and merely use faith on these things for ourselves. Revival is the **number one priority on God's agenda!** We should be working towards revival, interceding, believing and getting excited about a world-wide outpouring of revival fire!

> *'The Lord is not slack concerning His promise, as some men count slackness; but is longsuffering to us-ward, not willing that any should perish, **but that all should come to repentance.'*** (2 Pet 3:9)

God's heartbeat is that the whole world will come to Christ in these closing days of time before the return of Jesus Christ. Every Christian needs to be releasing their faith constantly towards revival by preparing themselves to be used, talking about it, evangelising, encouraging others to believe for revival and hungering for it in the light of today's society. Britain **needs revival**. It is up to the church to pray in faith for this to come to pass. Britain shall be saved to the glory of God.

From Faith to Faith

> *'For therein is the righteousness of God revealed **from faith to faith**: as it is written. The just shall live by faith.'* (Rom 1:17)

Faith is a developing process. Every believer is at a different level of faith. God knows each believer's heart and will only allow things to happen to us that our faith can cope with. God uses various trials and circum-stances, however, in our lives to cause faith to grow even more. The next time you are faced with a seemingly insurmountable trial just say: 'Praise God, here is another opportunity for my faith to grow.' That is a victorious attitude. I am glad that Paul writes:

> *'There hath no temptation taken you but such as is common to man: but God is **faithful**, who will not suffer you to be tempted above that ye are able: but will with the temptation also make **a way to escape**, that **ye may be able to bear it**.'*　　(1 Cor 10:13)

I have had to use this verse many times to assure myself and gain faith in times of severe testing. Our faith cannot remain stagnant. It must grow and develop. We must take all the 'steps' of faith that come our way to arrive at the kind of faith that Jesus used (Ps 37:23–24). The psalmist says later:

> *'They that go down to the sea in ships, that do business in great waters: These see the works of the LORD, and **His wonders in the deep**.'*　　(Ps 107:23–24)

Once we find ourselves in shallow water we need to get back into deep water because that is where the miracles are. Jesus told Peter: *'Launch out into the **deep**'* (Lk 5:4) and what a miracle he saw! As soon as God calls us to go into deep waters three forces are almost immediately activated. **Doubt**, **fear** and **unbelief**. We must use our faith to destroy all three and to say with Joshua and Caleb:

> *'... Let us go up at once, and possess it: for **we are well able to overcome it**.'*　　(Num 13:30)

– Faith turns wimps into warriors.
– Faith makes champions out of failures.
– Faith says yes to impossibilities.
– Faith converts dreams into realities.

- The life of faith is never boring but is always on the look-out for the next challenge to flex its muscles.
- Faith is aggressive and keeps on fighting until it wins.
- Faith **never gives up** but says: **'I will ... until.'** Hallelujah!

Chapter 10

Delegate or Stagnate

One person can only be in one place at a time doing one thing. You would think that is a superfluous statement. However, this statement needs to be **bellowed** into the ears of many Christians, particularly pastors and leaders. Pastors are the most guilty of all for violating this incredibly simple, yet profound scriptural truth. One person can only effectively handle, and care for, a few people. Jesus only had 12! Paul the Apostle teaches the church at Ephesus a very clear instruction in church leadership which needs careful application for every church. In fact, it is one of the major factors to assist church growth.

> *'And He gave some, apostles; some, prophets; and some, evangelists; and some, pastors and teachers: For the perfecting of the saints, **for the work of the ministry**, for the edifying of the body of Christ.'*
>
> (Eph 4:11, 12)

Let me ask you a question. Who is supposed to do the **work of the ministry**? This verse (verse 12) tells us that it is the saints who do – having been trained and perfected by the five-fold ministry! This is confirmed in the Acts of the Apostles:

> *'And in those days, when the number of the disciples was multiplied, there arose a murmuring of the Grecians against the Hebrews, because their widows were neglected in the daily ministration. Then the twelve called the multitude of the disciples unto them, and said, It is not reasonable that we should leave the Word of God and serve tables. Wherefore, brethren, look ye out among you seven men of honest report, full of the Holy Ghost and wisdom, whom we may appoint over this business. But we will give ourselves continually to prayer, and to the ministry if the word.'*
> (Acts 6:1–4, read to verse 8)

If only churches could realise this vital truth of sharing out duties. Remember that every time you do something which somebody else could be doing, you are causing not one but **two** negatives against the growth of the church. Firstly, you are depriving someone in the Body who probably wants to do a job for the Lord. This often results in that person becoming critical and bitter (check your own church!). Secondly, by doing a job that some-one else could and should be doing, you are using time that could be used to **fulfil the high call of God on your life**. If you are in leadership you should be spending your time fasting, praying and studying the Word and waiting for the next instruction from Father. Then, when you have heard from Him you can then motivate the Body to fulfil what God has said to you.

One of the reasons why we are so reluctant to let go of anything is that we do not trust the people to do as good a job as we could! This is called **pride**. You will find that some within the Body will do a **better job than you could!**

These people, however, may never get the chance to discover their giftings.

If you are not in leadership within your church then go to the leaders and ask for something to do. If I were you I would keep on pestering them until you are given a job! If everyone in the Body was doing what they should be, then nobody would be overbusy or underbusy. Everyone would be fulfilled and there would be no 'burn-outs' or 'dry-ups'. This is what God has ordained for His Church.

Let me tell you what will happen if you do not use the gifts in your church. Those people will eventually become discouraged and either become a negative influence in your church or go and join another church where their ministries can be properly harnessed and brought to maturity. You rarely find a person who is fulfilling his ministry becoming discouraged. He is usually happy and positive and above all a positive influence which filters throughout the church.

Round Pegs in Round Holes

We need to make a note here regarding the principle of delegation. The whole process will only work if you have the right people doing the right jobs! Stagnation will soon appear in a church where people are doing the wrong jobs! Round pegs only fit into round holes. This often involves patience and praying the right people into key positions. Never begin a ministry without an anointed person to carry it forward. This is easier said than done. A good example of this is a youth ministry which is a specialised ministry and calling. Just because you need a youth group doesn't mean that you should have one. Firstly, pray for a youth leader with an anointing for that job. Then the group will flourish, particularly if the leader is hearing from heaven! Having said this I do appreciate that some ministries within the church have to be done even if we do not have the right people yet!

Jesus the Master Delegator

The story of Jesus feeding the multitude with a few fish and a small portion of bread is mentioned in all four gospels (Mt 14:21; 15:38; Mk 8:9; Lk 9:14; Jn 6:10). In this story we see the Son of God setting an example to us all of sharing and delegation. So many of us need to recognise this simple revelation in everyday life as well as in our work and especially ministry. All too often someone gets a job and holds onto it and is reluctant to allow anybody else near it! This is so sad because it stagnates the body eventually. The problem is magnified when that person is away and nobody does that job! This happens regularly and causes unneccessary heartache to leaders in particular. We **must learn to share** and **train others to do what we are doing**. Jesus did and expects us to. Paul says:

> *'And the things that thou hast heard of me among many witnesses, the same commit thou to faithful men, who shall be able to teach others also.'*
>
> (2 Tim 2:2)

This verse paints a vivid picture of how a multiplying church should run. **Duplication** plus **delegation** leads to **growth**.

Satan has done a good job to prevent this through **pride of position**. Jesus knows that He would be silly to try to feed 5000 people besides women and children on His own. Let us look closely at what He does.

> *'And he commanded them to make all sit down by companies upon the green grass. And they sat down in ranks, by hundreds, and by fifties.'* (Mk 6:39, 40)

Matthew gives us a little bit more detail by saying:

> *'And he commanded the multitude to sit down on the grass, and took the five loaves and the two fishes, and looking up to heaven, he blessed, and brake, and gave the loaves to His disciples, and the disciples to the multitude.'* (Mt 14:19)

Jesus only physically gives food to 12 men! How many Christians, leaders in particular, have worn themselves out by doing far too many things they were not called to do in the first place. Even now I still find myself doing things that I know I should share with others. We must share if we are going to see the growth and ultimate revival that God has promised in these last days.

In the first eight chapters of Luke's gospel, we see Jesus ministering to many people and teaching everywhere He went. His disciples probably watched Him like a hawk in everything that he did. Nobody had ever done such things before. Jesus pours His life into His disciples and then He releases them into ministry as well.

> *'Then he called his twelve disciples together, and gave them power and authority over all devils, and to cure diseases. And he sent them to preach the kingdom of God, and to heal the sick.'* (Lk 9:1–2)

Jesus could have carried on for a whole three and a half years on His own up to Calvary and His disciples would only have been **spectators** instead of **participators**!

133

You learn far more when you can actually do something instead of just watching someone else. Jesus trusted this bunch of weaklings even though they all deserted Him a short while later! Jesus knew that He could train these men on the job and that He would be there as their consultant and on-going trainer.

In Chapter 10 of Luke's gospel we see Jesus release 70 other people into the ministry and give them all good advice for their travelling (verses 1–12). We see these 70 reporting back to Jesus after their first attempts on their own.

> *'And the seventy returned again with joy, saying, Lord, even the devils are subject unto us through thy name.'* (Lk 10:17)

Jesus never misses an opportunity to teach them and is quick to notice pride over deliverance ministry and warn them not to rejoice in the power over evil spirits but to keep their eyes on Him (verses 18–20).

We must learn to trust people and give them a gentle push into things for the first time. People are almost always reluctant to have 'a go' at a new area of ministry. Jesus was never reserved about throwing people into the deep end and we shouldn't be either. You don't know that you can do something until **you try**. Most of us make mistakes the first time we do anything. We learn from our mistakes. It is pride that says 'I don't want to do that in case I make a mistake.' This is something which we all have to overcome if we are to be useful in God's service. God is more patient with **effort** than He is with **laziness** and **lethargy**. Remember that you are not on your own when you do anything for the Lord. The Spirit of Truth is with us to lead and guide us. God help us to realise the biblical principle of delegation before stagnation creeps in and stifles any growth.

Jethro Confronts Moses

Moses is a mighty man of God who has been carefully prepared (in the wilderness) for divine service. He has been called at the famous burning bush (Ex 3:2). What a shame that he lacks common sense. We sometimes think that God will tell us everything by revelation. This is not the case. God did not remove our brains when we entered service for the Lord! You would think so however, when you see Moses in this situation!

> *'And it came to pass on the morrow, that Moses sat to judge the people: and the people stood by Moses from the morning to the evening. And when Moses' father-in-law saw all that he did to the people, he said, what is this thing that thou doest to the people? Why sittest thou thyself alone, and all the people stand by thee from morning unto even? And Moses said unto his father-in-law, Because the people come unto me to inquire of God: When they have a matter, they come unto me: and I judge between one and another, and I do make them know the statutes of God, and His laws. And Moses' father-in-law said unto him, **the thing that thou doest is not good. Thou wilt surely wear away, both thou, and this people** that is with thee: **For this thing is too heavy for thee: Thou art not able to perform it thyself alone.**'*

(Ex 18:13–18)

Every pastor in the world should take very careful note of what Jethro then says:

> *'Hearken now unto my voice, I will give thee counsel, and God shall be with thee: Be thou for the people to Godward, that thou mayest bring the causes unto God: And thou shalt teach them ordinances and*

135

*laws, and shalt shew them the way wherein they must walk, and the work that they must do. Moreover thou shalt provide **out of the people** able men, such as fear God, men of truth, hating covetousness: and place such over them, to be **rulers of thousands**, and **rulers of hundreds**, **rulers of fifties**, and **rulers of tens**: And let them judge the people **at all seasons**: and it shall be, **that every great matter** they shall bring unto thee, but **every small matter they shall judge**: So shall it be easier for thyself, and **they shall bear the burden with thee**.'*

(Ex 18:19–22, see also verses 23–26)

Moses realises how preposterous this situation is and acts immediately on the wise counsel of Jethro. Moses was heading for disaster very quickly! Let us all meditate on these powerful Scriptures and mature in our ministries at every level of Christian service. Delegate or stagnate!

Delegation and the Trinity

We all know that God is omnipresent, that is He is everywhere all at once and knows exactly what is happening in everybody's life the world over. There are, however, three persons in the Godhead: Father, Son and Holy Spirit, each person having a different function within the Trinity and there are Cherubim and Seraphim, Archangels and angels who hearken unto God's Word. The principle of delegation has thus been around for much longer than creation itself. This is the way that our great God operates all the time. It is about time then that we all learn to share, train, delegate and release people constantly to promote accelerated growth right through the ranks of any church. If we 'hog' ministries we prevent others from the joy that we experience (Luke 10:17, the disciples *'returned with joy'*). Also, the devil will play on our ego and we become puffed up and good for nothing.

Delegate or stagnate!

Chapter 11

Prayer, Fasting and Spiritual Warfare

The Word of God shows clearly that there are different kinds of prayer for different reasons and purposes that we encounter in life (Eph 6:18, 19; 1 Tim 2:1–2 for example). The purpose of this chapter is to give a brief introduction to praying and does not cover all that the Bible says about the subject.

Devotional Praying

> *'As the hart panteth after the water brooks, so panteth my soul after thee, O God. My soul thirsteth for God, for the living God: When shall I come and appear before God?'*　　　　　　　　(Ps 42:1–2)

Probably the most important ingredient in developing an effective personal prayer life is simply devoting our love, passion and heart to our Father. We should spend time in His presence simply to tell Him that we love Him. Nothing delights the Father more than to be told that we love Him with all our hearts.

I love you Father for who you are.
I love you my Lord for always being there.
I love you Jesus for dying for me.

I love you Jesus for setting me free.
I love you Lord with all my heart.
I love you for forgiving me.
I love you and I want to love you more.
I love you for all that you have done for me.
I love you for what you are doing in my life now.
I love you for never letting me go.

One young lady who had recently found Christ as her personal Saviour was attending a crusade meeting. At the end of the meeting she went to the front of the church and knelt down and prayed these words:

'I love you Lord and I want to love you more.
I love you Lord and I want to love you more.'

She kept on saying these words for several hours after the meeting. That woman later became a missionary! The love and passion that developed between her and the Lord grew so close through her devotional life that God called her into Divine service for Him. Let me tell you what happens when you devote yourself to God like this woman did. The relationship between you and God becomes so close and intimate that the Lord Himself begins to talk to you as a friend and gives you His plans and purposes directly from the throne room.

Prayer is two-way communication between us and God. When we live a close devotional life with our Heavenly Father we tune in to His voice in a much clearer way. This brings delight to God and He rewards us accordingly. Moses was a man who lived close to the Lord by spending much quality time in His presence.

*'(Now the man **Moses** was very meek, above all the men which were upon the face of the earth.) And the Lord spake suddenly unto Moses, and unto*

*Aaron, and unto Miriam, come out ye three unto the tabernacle of the congregation. And they three came out. And the Lord came down in the pillar of the cloud, and stood in the door of the tabernacle, and called Aaron and Miriam: and they both came forth. And he said, Hear now my words: If there be a prophet among you, I the Lord will make myself known unto him in a vision, and will speak unto him in a dream. My servant Moses is not so, who is faithful in all mine house. **With him I will speak mouth to mouth**, even apparently, and not in dark speeches; and the similitude of the Lord shall he behold: Wherefore then were ye not afraid to speak against my servant Moses?'* (Num 12:3–8)

The more we spend time in devotion with the Lord the more He opens unto us His heart. He wants us to love Him just for Him. It is true that He wants to answer our prayers and provide for us but if this is the only reason why we are serving Him then we are missing that deep intimate relationship with Him as a person, friend and Father. He loves you and desires that you spend regular quality time lingering and basking in His lovely presence:

*'Be still, and know that **I am God**.'* (Ps 46:10)

'The secret of the Lord is with them that fear him: and he will show them his covenant.' (Ps 25:14)

*'Thou wilt show me the path of life: **in thy presence is fulness of joy**: at thy right hand there are pleasures for evermore.'* (Ps 16:11)

I have personally sensed the presence of God in a greater way when I have been dwelling in His presence just telling Him how much I love Him. He waits patiently for us to **make the time** to meet with Him. We sometimes find ourselves in a rut with our quiet times. If this is the case then we need to have the self-discipline to break out of the routine and do something different to bring back the sparkle in our relationship. I find that going for a long walk in the countryside and praying is best for me. We all have to find out what works for us. I remember hearing one godly man say that the only way that he could obtain peace and quiet each morning was to lock himself in the toilet and cry out to God!

> '*Draw nigh* (close) *to God, and he will draw nigh* (close) *to you.*' (Jas 4:8a)

God has secrets that He wants to share with each of us as individuals:

> '*The secret things belong unto the Lord our God: but those* **things which are revealed belong to us and to our children** *for ever, that we may do all the words of this law.*' (Deut 29:29)

These secrets are lovingly despatched to us when we take the time to search for God with all our hearts.

> '*And ye shall seek me, and find me, when ye shall search for me with all your heart.*' (Jer 29:13)

This devotional life is an absolute prerequisite to a highly fruitful all-round prayer life. It forms the basis for all that we do in His name. What we do **for Him** must come out of **our relationship with Him**.

Praise and Worship

Whenever praise and worship is mentioned most Christians immediately think of Sunday morning or some

141

other church meeting. The Bible makes it quite clear, however, that praise and worship should be a lifestyle. We should be praising and worshipping God all the time! Many Christians who become sad, depressed and miserable during the week are just about breaking through in to joy by the end of Sunday morning meeting, when it is time to go home again! When are we going to discipline ourselves to put on the garments of praise and to **keep them on**?

> *'By him therefore let us offer the sacrifice of praise to God **continually**, that is, the **fruit of our lips, giving thanks to his name**.'*   (Heb 13:15)

> *'**I will** bless the **Lord at all times**: His praise shall **continually be in my mouth**.'*   (Ps 34:1)

Continually means constantly, regularly, always and perpetually. No wonder Paul the apostle says:

> *'rejoice in the Lord **alway**: and **again I say, rejoice**.'*
> (Phil 4:4)

He goes on to say:

> *'Rejoice evermore. Pray **without ceasing**. In every thing give thanks: for this is the will of God in Christ Jesus concerning you.'*   (1 Thess 5:16–18)

If you want to lead a totally victorious Christian life then you need to give yourself to constant praise and worship out of sheer love and adoration to the Lord.

> *'But the hour cometh, and now is, when the true worshippers shall worship the Father in spirit and in truth: for the Father seeketh such to worship him.*

> *God is a spirit: and they that worship him must worship him in spirit and in truth.'*   (Jn 4:23–24)

Habakkuk knew the power of praise even though everything was seemingly falling apart:

> *'Although the fig tree shall not blossom, neither shall fruit be in the vines: the labour of the olive shall fail, and the fields shall yield no meat: the flock shall be cut off from the fold, and there shall be no herd in the stalls: **yet I will rejoice in the Lord. I will joy in the God of my salvation**. The LORD God is my strength, and **he will make my feet like hind's feet, and he will make me to walk upon mine high places**. To the chief singer on my stringed instruments.'*

> (Hab 3:17)

What tremendous faith Habakkuk had! It is easy to praise and rejoice when everything looks good, but we are a people of faith who trust God at all times and praise Him even if the circumstances look disastrous. Faith and praise are married. Worry and praise have never been married. It is impossible to rejoice in the Lord when you are worrying about something! Worry is a lack of trust in God to see you through. Nehemiah tells us:

> *'... Neither be ye sorry: for **the joy of the Lord is your strength**.'*   (Neh 8:10b)

Once you have lost your joy you will lose your strength and become sad, miserable, depressed and **a tool for the devil**! This is why we must keep praising all the time because continual praise produces joy which gives us strength to crush down our enemies. Hallelujah!

- Get up in the morning and rejoice.
- Go out of the house rejoicing.
- Rejoice in the car all the way to work.
- Keep rejoicing all day at work.
- Come home rejoicing.
- Go to bed praising and rejoicing.

As you rejoice all the time you will notice how fruitful your life will become for the Lord. God will then take you higher and higher in your service for Him.

I remember hearing a story once of a pastor who was thrown into prison for preaching the gospel. For 18 hours a day he was immersed up to his neck in human excrement. He found himself complaining to the Lord and asking Him why this was happening to him. God spoke to him and told him to rejoice in this situation. The man began to praise God each day amidst the stench and filth of this unpleasant situation. After a short while he was inexplicably released from prison! He had learnt to praise God in probably the worst situation that he could find himself in. Remind yourself of this pastor the next time you want to gripe, complain and feel sorry for yourself!

*'To appoint unto them that mourn in Zion, to give unto them beauty for ashes, the oil of **joy** for mourning, **the garments of praise for the spirit of heaviness**: that they might be called trees of righteousness, the planting of the LORD, that he might be glorified.'*

(Is 61:3)

*'And at midnight Paul and Silas prayed, and sang praises unto God: and the prisoners heard them. And suddenly there was a great earthquake, so that the foundations of the prison were shaken: and immediately all the doors were opened, and **every one's bands were loosed**.'* (Acts 16:25–26)

144

When are we going to learn to praise at all times and in every situation?

> *'Oh that men would praise the Lord for his goodness, and for his wonderful works to the children of men!'*
> (Ps 107:8, 15, 21, 31)

Praying for Things

> *'But seek ye **first** the kingdom of God, and his righteousness: and all **these things** shall be added unto you.'*
> (Mt 6:33)

We are living in a physical world handling material things every day of our lives. Jesus is talking here about material things such as food and clothing. His promise is that if we put God and His work first then He will supply *'all our needs according to His riches in glory!'* (Phil 4:19).

Jesus then says in John's gospel:

> *'And in that day ye shall ask me nothing. Verily, verily, I say unto you, whatsoever ye shall ask the Father in my name, he will give it you. Hitherto have ye asked nothing in my name: ask, and ye shall receive, that your joy may be full.'* (Jn 16:23–24)

This verse and others like it teach us that we are meant to ask for things in the material or spiritual world and expect God to answer. It is interesting to note that God only gives us general guidelines for such praying and leaves the responsibility upon us as to what we ask for! James gives us some serious advice on such praying:

> *'Ye lust, and have not: ye kill, and desire to have, and cannot obtain: ye fight and war, yet ye have not,*

145

*because ye ask not. Ye ask, and receive not, because
ye ask amiss, that ye may consume it upon your lusts.'*
(Jas 4:2–3)

If we are asking for things in the material world purely
out of self-indulgence and the lusts of the flesh then God
will not answer us. All such praying ought to be for
genuine needs that we have that we cannot naturally
afford. For instance, in the day and age that we are
living in a motor car is an essential item. I have personally seen God provide in this way, and when God
provides a car it is paid for!

How do we go about praying for things?

*'Therefore I say unto you, what **things** soever ye
desire, when ye pray, believe that ye receive them, and
ye shall have them.'*　　　　　　　　　　(Mk 11:24)

When you are praying for material things you only
need to pray and ask once. God hears you the first time.
Then we are to believe that we receive them. This is the
most important time because we must then thank God
for answering our prayer and praise Him for the thing
we have asked for until we see it manifest. You may ask
the question 'How long does it take?' The answer is quite
simple. Until you see what you prayed for! When a
farmer sows a seed in the ground he does not go around
in a panic wondering how long it is going to take before
his harvest comes. He knows that different seeds take
different lengths of time to produce.

It is the same with praying for things. Some things
take months, sometimes years, but some things take only
minutes, even seconds.

I have used this kind of prayer thousands of times (I
use this kind of prayer several times a day), and sometimes the prayer is only just out of my lips when I see

what I have prayed for. In the light of the fact that some things take time to manifest I don't wait until I am desperately in need of that item! I pray months (even years) in advance for some items that we need. For example, holidays. My wife and I pray for an annual two-week holiday in the summer. We usually pray for the next holiday when we arrive back from the last one. In the early years our faith would often be stretched to the limit as we would have to wait up to the last minute for a holiday. Now the blessing has overtaken us! For the last couple of years we have hardly had to mention a holiday to the Lord and He has provided us with one. Praise the Lord!

Once you have asked for what you want you then have to trust God about the way in which it may come. Don't try to work it out for yourself. God has so many creative ways to provide for us. I was once in a situation where God had told me to book an expensive hall for a series of meetings. The big problem was that we had to pay one month in advance! I had no money at all. A lady, who knew absolutely nothing about this situation came to our house three days before this bill was due. She handed me a brown envelope and told me to open it after she had gone. There in this envelope was the exact amount of the bill; £493 in £20 notes, £10 notes, £5 and pound coins. I could never have worked out where and how that money was going to come. How our Father provides for something is His business. Just allow Him to do things His way.

We have used this kind of praying for every aspect of life. Food, clothing, cars, holidays, airline tickets, homes, rent etc. I once went into a shop with my wife and two children to buy the children some clothes. We came out of the shop with our merchandise and more money than we went in with! God sent someone into the shop and they gave us some money which was more than we spent on the clothes. God cares about every detail of our lives and wants us to acknowledge Him in all that we do. I even pray this kind of prayer when driving to find a parking place or to get out onto a busy road. It always works!

> *'And he said unto them, Take heed, and beware of covetousness: for man's life consisteth not in the abundance of the things which he possesseth. And he spake a parable unto them, saying, The ground of a certain rich man brought forth plentifully: And he thought within himself, saying, What shall I do, because I have no room where to bestow my fruits? And he said, This will I do: I will pull down my barns, and build greater: and there will I bestow all my fruits and my goods. And I will say to my soul, soul, thou hast much goods laid up for many years: take thine ease, eat, drink, and be merry. But God said unto him, Thou fool, this night thy soul shall be required of thee: then whose shall those things be, which thou hast provided? So is he that layeth up treasure for himself, and is not* **rich toward God.***'*   (Lk 12:15–21)

God is not against us having **things**, He is against **things** having a hold of us!

A Lifestyle of Fasting

Many Christians are struggling in their spiritual lives because they have never taken fasting seriously. I heard someone say recently that they had been in a church for about three years and had never heard fasting mentioned from the leadership. What a tragedy.

After the first 30 years of Jesus' life He began His three and a half year ministry. The very first thing that He did before ministering to anybody, immediately after He was baptised in water and the Spirit was to fast:

> *'Then was Jesus led up of the Spirit into the wilderness to be tempted of the devil. And when he had **fasted** forty days and forty nights, he was afterward an hungered.'* (Mt 4:1–2)

If Jesus needed to fast before He ministered then we certainly need to! Later on in Matthew Jesus gives some teaching on fasting:

> *'And Jesus said unto them, can the children of the bridechamber mourn, as long as the bridegroom is with them? but the days will come, when the bridegroom shall be taken from them, and **then shall they fast**.'* (Mt 9:15)

Also, He takes it for granted that everybody will fast by saying:

> *'Moreover **when ye fast**, be not, as the hypocrites, of a sad countenance: for they disfigure their faces, that they may appear unto men to fast. Verily I say unto you, They have their reward.'* (Mt 6:16)

This verse does not say **'if you fast'** but **'when you fast'**. Fasting is not an option but a requirement for true Christian discipleship and especially Christian ministry. How a person can fulfil their call without regular times of fasting and prayer remains a mystery.

When we come to the area of deliverance ministry, fasting is an absolute requirement for Jesus said:

> *'Howbeit this kind goeth not out but by prayer **and fasting**.'* (Mt 17:21)

Notice how all the modern translations have carefully removed the word 'fasting' from this and other verses of Scripture.

Satan does not want deliverance restored to the church! However, he is in for a surprise because it is coming back to the church in a mighty way. The following passage of Scripture needs careful study by every serious Christian and should be read regularly throughout life.

> *'Is not this the fast that I have chosen? to **loose the bands of wickedness**, to **undo the heavy burdens**, and to **let the oppressed go free**, and **that ye break every yoke?** Is it not to deal thy bread to the hungry, and that thou bring the poor that are cast out to thy house? When thou seest the naked, that thou cover him: and that thou hide not thyself from thine own flesh? **Then shall thy light break forth as the morning**, and **thine health shall spring forth speedily:** and **thy righteousness shall go before thee:** the **glory of the Lord** shall be thy rearward* (Guard you from behind). *Then shalt thou call, and **the Lord shall answer:** thou shalt cry, and He shall say, Here I am. If thou take away from the midst of thee the yoke, the putting forth of the finger, and **speaking vanity;** And if thou draw out thy soul to the hungry, and satisfy the afflicted soul: then **shall thy light rise in obscurity**, and thy darkness be as the noonday: **and the Lord shall guide thee continually**, and satisfy thy soul in drought, and make fat thy bones; and thou shalt be like a watered garden, and like a spring of water, whose waters fail not. And they that shall be of thee shall build the old waste places: thou shalt raise up the foundations of many generations; and thou shalt be called, The repairer of the breach, the restorer of paths to dwell in.'* (Is 58:6–12)

Let us summarise the benefits of fasting.
1.   It looses the bands of wickedness.
2.   It will undo the heavy burdens.
3.   It lets the oppressed go free.
4.   It breaks every yoke.
5.   It enables you to feed the poor.
6.   It helps you to clothe those who are naked.
7.   It enables you to provide for your own family.
8.   It causes your light to break forth.
9.   It speeds up your healing.
10. It makes righteousness go before you.
11. It allows the glory of the LORD to be a shield behind you.
12. It causes God to hear and answer your prayers.
13. It guarantees guidance all the time throughout life.
14. It causes you to be provided for in recession.
15. It makes you like a watered garden (i.e. fruitful).
16. It brings renewal, restoration, revival and reformation.

I trust that you will now go into your prayer closet and repent of not taking fasting seriously and **begin now**.

Praying in Other Tongues

'And these signs shall follow them that believe: In my name shall they cast out devils; they shall speak with new tongues.'   (Mk 16:17)

'He that speaketh in an unknown tongue edifieth himself; but he that prophesieth edifieth the church.'
(1 Cor 14:4)

'I thank my God, I speak with tongues more than ye all.'   (1 Cor 14:18)

No wonder Paul the Apostle had an abundance of revelations! (2 Cor 12:7). Anyone who prays for long periods in tongues will begin to break into new depths in the spirit realm.

There are different stages that we go through in our development in tongues. Firstly, when we first begin to speak in tongues we are praising and worshipping God and edifying ourself. With our known language we are very limited in what we can say to God in praise. In tongues, however, we can go on exalting, praising and worshipping our God in all kinds of languages. It is truly wonderful to be able to magnify our Father for all His goodness to us in this God-given way. However, this is only the beginning of an exciting new world of prayer. Praise and worship are just the start.

When I first started to speak in tongues I only had about two words for three weeks. I kept repeating them until the breakthrough came and the rivers started! I prayed much in tongues and God kept adding new words each week. Paul talks about *'singing in the spirit'* (1 Cor 14:15). I found this quite difficult to begin with but eventually broke through. This can be done publicly and privately. In Romans we read:

> *'Likewise the spirit also helpeth our infirmities: for we know not what we should pray for as we ought; but the spirit itself maketh intercession for us with groanings which cannot be uttered. And he that searcheth the hearts knoweth what is the mind of the spirit, because he maketh intercession for the saints according to the will of God.'* (Rom 8:26–27)

This reveals the next stage of praying in tongues. When we pray in tongues for a period of time we will discover the intercessory languages of the spirit. These are different languages from our praise tongue. When we are just starting we have to persevere until we break through into these languages. The devil does not want you to find these other tongues so you have to pray in tongues until you discover them. It took my wife about nine months to break through into these intercessory prayer languages. Don't give up until you find them yourself.

When I started many years ago I set myself a target of 30 minutes the first day, then 35 minutes the next day and built it up each day. Evenutally, I could pray in tongues for several hours at a time. As time went by I spent many hours in tongues. I discovered many intercessory prayer languages starting to develop. I knew in my spirit that I was really being used by God in deep intercession. Also, the Spirit of God would show me things to pray for in English. It was so exciting and still is. Prayer like this is never boring.

The Lord then moved me on to the next stage of praying in tongues – warfare in the heavenlies. There would be times when I would be praying in tongues and I would change from intercession to bold, aggressive praying with great authority. No wonder Paul says:

> *'For we wrestle not against flesh and blood, but against principalities, against powers, against the rulers of the darkness of this world, against spiritual wickedness in high* (heavenly) *places.'*   (Eph 6:12)

This is direct confrontation with the powers of darkness that hold individuals, villages, towns, cities and nations back from accepting Jesus as Lord (2 Cor 4:4). Once we begin opposing these demonic forces in the heavenlies the Holy Spirit begins to show us what we are dealing with, that is, He gives us the names of what we are dealing with so that we can cast them out. This is very similar to individual deliverance only on a larger scale.

If ever you find yourself praying like this then press in until you sense victory in your spirit. This is **real spiritual warfare** which brings about major changes in society and brings revival where there was barrenness. Hallelujah, God is wanting to recruit such intercessory prayer warriors to penetrate the darkness and usher in a mighty tidal wave of glory with revival ensuing. Will you take a step forward and be one more warrior for the Master? The pastor of the world's largest church says that there are three things that bring revival. Firstly, we are to pray. Secondly, we are to pray. Thirdly, we are to pray.

The Prayer Life of Jesus Christ

All that Jesus does in His earthly ministry is done to set us a wonderful example to follow (1 Pet 2:21). In the first epistle of John we read:

> *'He that saith he abideth in him ought himself also to walk, **even as he walked**.'* (1 Jn 2:6)

Jesus has left us an example of prayer that we should all take very seriously.

1. Jesus starts His ministry in the wilderness fasting and praying (Mt 4:1–11).
2. Jesus regularly retreats from the crowds to spend time with His Father (Lk 5:15–16).
3. Just before Calvary in the garden of Gethsemane He takes the time to pray (Mt 26:36–40). Verse 41 then reads:

> *'Watch **and pray**, that ye enter not into temptation: **the spirit indeed is willing**, but **the flesh is weak**.'*

4. On the cross itself we do not see Jesus moaning and having a pity party! Instead He prays for forgiveness for those blinded by sin (Lk 23:33–34).
5. Even today He is still praying and interceding for us! (Heb 7:25; 9:24)

154

If you desire to be used in the high calling of God then prayer must become the top priority in your life as it was and is in the life of Jesus Christ Himself.

When Jesus chose His twelve disciples He did not use a ballot box! What did He do? How did He know who to choose? Did He consult with the people? Did He go to the spiritual leaders of the day and ask advice? **No!** Let us see just exactly how the twelve came to be chosen.

> *'And it came to pass in those days, that he went out into a mountain to pray, and **continued all night in prayer to God.** And when it was day, he called unto him his disciples; and of them **he chose twelve**, whom also he named apostles.'* (Lk 6:12–13)

You will notice that the translators of the Bible have placed a new paragraph sign at the beginning of verse 13. However, the significance of these two verses being together is of paramount importance. Jesus knows that leaders are the key to the church and thus sets us a mandate for selecting the top leadership of the church. Note, people are not chosen as leaders for what they are but for **what they can become!** Study the life of Peter for instance! Jesus is so patient with him with all his faults, inadequacies and shortcomings. God knew that one day Peter would become the mighty man of faith and power and see 3000 people come to Christ in one message! (Acts 2:41). No wonder the Holy Spirit inspires Paul to write these words:

> *'Be careful for nothing* (careful means anxious or worried)*; but in **every thing** by prayer and supplication with thanksgiving let your requests be made known unto God.'* (Phil 4:6)

Jesus adopts this policy in His earth walk on numerous occasions by offering up simple, short prayers to the Father. Jesus walks in total consistent fellowship with the Father through prayer. He does nothing by Himself that is independent from the Father's will. We need to discipline ourselves to develop the same kind of close personal fellowship with God whatever we are doing in the Kingdom of God. By staying close to God in prayer we will be more likely to hear His instructions to us. The less we pray the more we are likely to do our own thing and end up **striving**. The people who hear from God are those who walk with God.

One of the things that I do regularly and have done for about two years is to go away for four days at a time four times a year. I find personally that I can pray more easily when away from my 'war zone'. I never fail to hear the next instruction clearly. We all need to build something like this into our own life. I realise that we cannot all do what I do but God understands your limitations and will provide for you to suit your circumstances. We are all different so find out what works for you.

Finally, I challenge you to read carefully John chapter 17 all the way through and ask God to reveal to you by the Holy Spirit many of the ingredients of successful praying. Pay attention to what Jesus prays for and what He doesn't pray for! Make a list of all the valuable revelations that Jesus mentions and start to apply them to your own prayer life.

For further information on books, tapes, videos or the Ministry, please write to:

Life Changing Ministries
Bemersley House
Gitana Street
Hanley
Stoke on Trent
ST1 1DY
UK